Advance Praise for *Love That Works*

"Bruce Brander has written an absolutely splendid book which highlights the many problems associated with a culture that primarily thinks of love in the context of fleeting romantic attractions. . . . Like a good physician, Brander offers a cure in the form of a much broader concept of love."

> —Dr. Stephen G. Post, professor of biomedical ethics, Case Western Reserve University, and president of the Institute for Research on Unlimited Love

"I have over thirty books in my personal library that deal with some aspect of love and without any exaggeration this is one of the finest I have read. . . . This book will become required reading for my students. I know that anybody who wants to experience love at deeper, richer, and more meaningful levels will clearly benefit from . . . [this] wonderful and much-needed book."

> —Dr. Gary J. Oliver, executive director of the Center for Marriage and Family Studies and professor of psychology and practical theology at John Brown University

"What is most appealing and distinctive about [this] book is its emphasis on love as a high human endeavor and as an ethical discipline."

> —Dr. Barbara Dafoe Whitehead, co-director of the National Marriage Project, Rutgers University

"*Love That Works* is a lively, well-crafted text that delves into the rich, multiple meanings of love. . . . Unsurprisingly, many of Brander's sources fall within, or grow out of, the Christian tradition. But this is a book for everyone."

> —Dr. Jean Bethke Elshtain, professor of social and political ethics, University of Chicago

your mind and touch your heart. You owe it to yourself—and your love
life—to read this book."
—Dr. Les and Dr. Leslie Parrott, co-directors, Center for Relationship
Development, department of psychology, Seattle Pacific University,
and authors of *Saving Your Marriage Before It Starts*

"Provocative and lively, [*Love That Works*] ranges widely over many disciplines and historical sources. I think many people, especially the young, will benefit from [its] thoughtful analysis of love.... I read [*Love That Works*] as a study on how to produce *complete love.*"
—Dr. Steven L. Nock, professor of sociology, University of Virginia,
and director of Marriage Matters

"Mr. Brander brings a varied and rich background to his examination of the way we love.... he places our current problems of loving in context so that we can understand how we got here. Then he offers suggestions as to how to love so that it works, it lasts. A message for our particular time."
—Dr. Katherine Spaht, professor of law, Louisiana State
University at Baton Rouge, and drafter of Louisiana's
1997 covenant marriage legislation

"*Love That Works* will make a significant and well-received contribution to the contemporary discussion of relationship and marriage.... This book can provide essential background to those studying relationships in their own lives and in our society. *Loves That Works* also will provide hope and a vision."
—Dr. Barbara Markey, clinical psychologist specializing in
marriage and family counselling, and associate director,
Center for Marriage and Family at Creighton University

Love *That* Works

THE ART AND SCIENCE OF GIVING

Bruce Brander

TEMPLETON FOUNDATION PRESS
PHILADELPHIA AND LONDON

Templeton Foundation Press
Five Radnor Corporate Center, Suite 120
100 Matsonford Road
Radnor, Pennsylvania 19087
www.templetonpress.org

Templeton Foundation Press helps intellectual leaders and others learn about science research on aspects of realities, invisible and intangible. Spiritual realities include unlimited love, accelerating creativity, worship, and the benefits of purpose in persons and in the cosmos.

Designed and typeset by Gopa & Ted2, Inc.
Illustrations: Mary Brander

Library of Congress Cataloging-in-Publication Data

Brander, Bruce.
Love that works : the art and science of giving / Bruce Brander.
p. cm.
Includes bibliographical references and index.
ISBN 1-932031-77-4 (pbk. : alk. paper)
1. Love. 2. Man-woman relationships. I. Title.
BF575.L8B723 2004
152.4'1—dc22
2004014761

Printed in the United States of America

04 05 06 07 08   10 9 8 7 6 5 4 3 2 1

For Breton and Kerri Buckley
on their wedding day

Contents

Acknowledgments

I AM GRATEFUL to my wife Mary and to my friends Daryl Alder, Breton Buckley, Tony and Peg Krzyewski, and Brian Peterson for their generous help with this book. Their comments and encouragement proved immensely valuable.

I remain deeply grateful to the many eminent authorities who offered kind and encouraging comments and critiques for *Love That Works.* They include:

+ Alain de Botton, author of *On Love, The Romantic Movement, Kiss and Tell, Consolations of Philosophy,* and a director of the graduate philosophy program at London University
+ Dr. Jean Bethke Elshtain, Laura Spelman Rockefeller Professor of Social and Political Ethics at The University of Chicago
+ Dr. Norval D. Glenn, professor of sociology and American studies at the University of Texas in Austin
+ Dr. Vincent Jefferies, professor of sociology, California State University, Northridge
+ Robert F. Lehman, president of the Fetzer Institute of Kalamazoo, Michigan, one of the leading foundations supporting research, education, and service activities in the domain of mind, body, and spirit
+ Dana Mack, senior fellow at the Center for Education Studies and author of *The Assault on Parenthood: How Our Culture Undermines the Family,* and editor, with David Blankenhorn, of *The Book of Marriage: The Wisest Answers to the Toughest Questions*
+ Dr. Barbara Markey, clinical psychologist specializing in marriage and family counselling and associate director of the Center for Marriage and Family at Creighton University in Omaha, Nebraska

✦ Dr. David G. Myers, professor of social psychology at Hope College in Holland, Michigan

✦ Dr. Steven L. Nock, professor of sociology at the University of Virginia, Charlottesville, and director of Marriage Matters, an ongoing research project designed to find out what makes new marriages strong and healthy

✦ Dr. Gary J. Oliver, executive director of the Center for Marriage and Family Studies, professor of psychology and practical theology at John Brown University at Siloam, Arkansas, and author of numerous books

✦ Dr. Les Parrott, III, professor of clinical psychology and co-director of the Center for Relationship Development at Seattle Pacific University

✦ Dr. Leslie Parrott, marriage and family therapist and co-director of the Center for Relationship Development at Seattle Pacific University

✦ Dr. Stephen G. Post, professor of biomedical ethics in the school of medicine, Case Western Reserve University, and president of the Institute for Research on Unlimited Love, which studies altruism, compassion, and service

✦ Dr. Katherine Spaht, professor in the areas of family law, community property, successions and obligations at Louisiana State University and overseer for drafting Louisiana's covenant marriage legislation in 1997

✦ Dr. Barbara Dafoe Whitehead, sociologist, writer, and co-director of the National Marriage Project at Rutgers University, New Jersey

Part I

Love in the Dark

Love vs. Decency?

LOVE IS JUST A FOUR-LETTER WORD.
—BOB DYLAN

THE WAY WE LOVE

THE WAY WE LOVE is not working anymore. Hardly anyone will challenge that. Hard evidence convicts it in our lives, our hearts, our divorce courts.

Recalling author Kurt Vonnegut's wry appeal, "Please—a little less love, and a little more common decency," we might wonder if the way we love is really love at all. It feels so good then hurts so bad. It makes us happy then leaves us sad.

Many social scientists seriously question the validity of what we think of as love. Some scientific and religious thinkers refuse to call it love at all. Unstable, impractical, unreliable, the stuff of fantasy—these terms might describe our mode of loving better than any sweet nothings we might whisper.

We delight in the pleasures of romance, the most prominent kind of love in our time. Yet we also know that our mode of romance is a rough and rugged obstacle course that can sour, wound, embitter, cripple, and occasionally kill. Most of us personally have suffered sorrow, disappointment, and disillusion in our own romances. Anyone today embarking upon the perilous course of love feeling certain of happily-ever-after would seem either reckless or naive. Old-time hopes of life-long, loving bliss have turned unrealistic. Instead, we are guarded, suspicious, made so by what we see and experience of love.

Love has been exalted throughout the world's history as the answer to the problem of life. For us, love itself is the problem. We continue to believe that love is something we need, if not for raw survival than surely for a satisfying life. Yet we see love and its consequences tormenting people with some of the cruelest misfortunes of their lives. Most men and women are overwhelmingly convinced that existence without love is selfish, barren, pointless. They generally agree that love is life's greatest need, greatest hunger, greatest blessing. Yet to judge from the pains it inflicts, love commonly is life's greatest curse as well.

Because love's historic reputation proclaims it to be good, we often tend to think of it in ideal terms. We define love as nurturing, vital, beneficial, blissful, and a great many other lovely things—as church sermons exalt it, as the media promotes it, as love should be, or perhaps as it used to be.

Yet rarely does love in our society come close to matching the Bible's noble definition: patient, kind, not jealous, never rude, not self-seeking, never failing. Rarer still are the pyrotechnic passions of mass-media love, if they exist at all, with its popular fantasies of scorching sexuality and endless earthly euphoria.

Love as it should be? Well, we differ about that.

And love as it used to be, at least in people's minds: sweet and innocent, a dreamy sentiment, a lyrical flight of fancy, a many-splendored thing that some enchanted evening makes your heart go bumpitybump and your throat come up in a lump? Well, times have changed. People have changed. Love has changed.

Love has changed? Yes, absolutely. The nature of love and the way people do it changes in history from one period to another. In modern times, gradually, even imperceptibly, over only a few generations, our way of thinking about love and our manner of loving have mutated radically.

Modern changes in the way we love have reflected trends in the culture as a whole: from religious to secular; from duty-centered to self-centered; from humane to indifferent; from stress on responsibilities to emphasis on rights; from supportive community to impersonal society; from independent folk toward lockstep mass; from serving, contributing, and cooperating to competing, consuming, and regarding our fellows as things to be used or devoured.

Our society has gone far in reversing the normal, healthy way of human relationship based on mutual kindness and trust. Instead, we have come to accept as "normal" a system often based on mutual exploitation and self-defense.

Meanwhile, as psychoanalyst Erich Fromm observed, in any society love relationships are only a more intense expression of the culture's overall human dealings. In generations past, the romantic mode of love, tempered by moral considerations, was generally considerate, sweet, and faithful. Since then it has altered to emotionally uncontrolled, sexually hot, chancy, and often little more than another form of entertainment. Singles' bars, college campuses, movies, and women's magazines suggest that love for many lovers has diminished even further to the scratching of a sexual itch. Wherever we look we are likely to see love tainted with narcissism, emotional sterility, loneliness, bitterness, and peril.

Exploring Love's Basics

Though love in our time seems most conspicuous for its failure, we don't have to settle for that. There is no need to throw up our hearts in despair and resign our lives to emotional chance or chaos. Love should not threaten unutterable pain. Hearts were not made to be broken. No one should have to enter love without some reasonable guarantee of goodwill and stability.

We do have options, after all. We can, if we choose, in our personal lives, restore the glory to love and romance. We can seek, find, and practice a fuller kind of love that creates lasting benefits and offers fair assurance of permanence.

Granted, reinventing love completely is a task too daunting for any of us to undertake. Yet we can explore the basics of love in philosophy through the ages, in psychology both ancient and modern, in sociology, anthropology, and the world's great religious thinking. We can rediscover beneficial love for our time in the world's literature on love.

A lot of information awaits us, enough to give us a solid, fresh start. We will find, for example, a definitive answer to the question, "What is love?"—the most lucid answer given in all history, an ancient definition that has survived intact for more than 2,500 years. We will learn how to know for certain if we are in love and, more importantly, if love is in us. We will see how our failures in romance come from loving incompletely, in a fragmentary way. We will come to understand love as a natural progression, a spectrum, a continuum, a process of personal growth. We will find other, more effective ways to love, which we then can combine with romance for a fuller, total love. Finally, with our deeper knowledge of love, we can take steps to build successful love in our lives that will enrich not only ourselves but everyone around us.

Where shall we start? Perhaps before we consider more effective ways to love, we should gain a clearer understanding of the way we love now and why it is not working for us anymore.

———

Modern Romance

YUMMY, YUMMY, YUMMY (I'VE GOT LOVE IN MY TUMMY)
—OHIO EXPRESS BUBBLEGUM ROCK GROUP, 1968

IN THE MOOD

I F I FOLLOW the current ways of love, my romance is likely to go something like this.

I'm in the mood for love. I feel a hunger, a longing, an emptiness, a need. Unlike people of past generations, who found emotional support in a close community of relatives, friends, and neighbors, I live, as many people of the present, in relative emotional solitude.

I've been more or less persuaded by the society around me that "you're nobody until somebody loves you." So the first challenge of love, as I perceive it, is to find that Special Someone, a lover, companion, confidant, and soul mate, who can fill my empty heart to overflowing. I'm constantly on the lookout for my Special Person, perhaps without considering that what's missing in my life might be more about what's lacking in myself.

I might be looking for a date, perhaps for a mate. It doesn't matter which, as far as my methods are concerned.

I begin with a search. Opportunities are endless. We have Internet chat. We can scan the meet market of personal ads. For a fee we can select matching services, some especially designed for the young and lonely, for busy professionals, for widows and widowers, for Asian, black, Christian, or alternative; via telephone or online; with video introduction and personality tests; pre-screened and qualified, with photo and essay included. We might even seek a mail order bride (though not a groom) from Russia, Ukraine, the Philippines.

In my search for a partner, I behave like a savvy consumer on a shopping trip. I have definite specifications, which might include but not be limited to: gorgeous and brainy; tall and svelte; sweet and lovely; warm and amorous; classy and vivacious; funny and playful; a good conversationalist; likes travel, fine restaurants, sunsets, and fireside talks.

While no one would set such exacting standards for a relative, friend, teacher, or employer, a love partner must meet the most rigorous requirements. Yet I'm careful not to demand too much, aware of limitations in myself. As the nineteenth-century composer Robert Schumann recalled, "When I was a young man, I vowed never to marry until I found the ideal woman. Well I found her—but, alas, she was waiting for the ideal man."

With the marketing orientation that governs our culture and makes almost everything an object of exchange, I also experience myself as a commodity to be offered for consumption. I must sell myself, prove I am worthy of love. It's my job to charm, beguile, and entice potential partners.

To be lucky in love, I prepare. I bathe, deodorize, comb my hair, then comb it again hoping the sides will stay flat. I sort through my clothes, picking items for the image I intend to project. In a mirror I practice my casual smile and rehearse cool opening lines. I might watch television and read magazines, jotting down topics for intelligent conversation.

Like any salesman, I try to put together a package of qualities that potential buyers will find irresistible. Sometimes this involves false advertising, but that's all part of strong salesmanship. A psychologist might say that I feel inadequate as a person and long for someone to accept me and convince me I am relevant, even at the cost of forsaking sincerity and genuine intimacy. Be that as it may, I primp and preen to put on my very best front. If I have money, status, power, or vocational success—and perhaps even if I don't—I'll flaunt those as well.

While I dream of my ideal of femininity, my future Special Person is likely to be equally alone, lonely, and brimming with hope. She is readying for love in much the same way: adorning her figure in alluring clothes, styling her hair, making up her face, perfuming her ears, doing all she can to transform a day-to-day person into a gorgeous, sexy package. Of course, she, too, has a smart-shopper list of largely non-negotiable requirements for her ideal man, which I'll do my best to persuade her that I meet.

Both of us are trained to function in a culture where the aim of commerce is to make a good bargain: to get more than give, gain more than contribute, acquire more than bestow, accumulate more than disburse. As a consequence, we approach love more as consumers than producers. We long to acquire love but think less about giving it. Our hopes are fixed more on being loved than loving.

It hardly occurs to us to consider love as an inner activity rather than an external commodity, as an ability that resides, to greater or lesser degree, within ourselves. Even less do we see the need to develop emotional proficiencies and qualities of character that effective loving might require. Love, as we envision it, is *out there* somewhere. It is something to be found. To succeed in love, we must locate a supplier.

We assume that once we find our Special Someone we will simply fall in love. We will tumble into love passively, through no real choice of our own, like slipping on a banana peel or falling into a trance or a coma. When that happens, we will radiate love automatically in response, give it off like the sun sheds warmth, pour it forth like water from a spring.

We both understand that no serious endeavor in our society fails as often and dismally as romance. All our lives, all around us, we have witnessed sagging, crumbling, collapsing romantic relationships. We have heard enough stories of foundering love from relatives, friends, newspapers, magazines, songs, and movies to fill an encyclopedia of emotional misfortune. If we have any romantic experience at all, we probably have suffered similar failures of our own.

If a business venture, an educational endeavor, or an airplane trip held no more chance of success than romance, any sensible person would choose another course of action. Yet modern romance is the only way we know. So rarely do we question why so many people who fall in love also fail in love. Nor do we calculate ways to beat the odds. In a reckless triumph of hope over experience, we charge ahead, ignoring risk and uncertainty, full of confidence that somehow, for us, this time, things will be different.

TRUE ROMANCE

Suddenly I see her—across a crowded room, on a page of personal ads, over the infinity of cyberspace. With my eyes wide open I'm dreaming. She's beautiful, radiant, exquisite, everything I've ever hoped for.

As we meet, I'm bedazzled. Yet I'm careful not to seem too eager. I mentally review my coolest lines: "I've loved you since the beginning of time, and time began with you. . . . I saw you and was saved. . . . Swoon and I'll catch you." But this moment of reality seems to demand less: "Hi, I'm a Scorpio."

We chit-chat tensely, warily testing the water. I beam my broadest smile and try to look relaxed. I'm on my best behavior, projecting my chosen image. Observing myself critically as a member of my own audience, I put my most fetching traits on display and conceal anything that might show me in an unfavorable light. Sincerity and openness? Bad strategy! The game demands that we play one another like anglers.

Scanning her with my mental radar, I look for things to be agreeable about. My central message is: "I am what you want me to be." We perform like actors auditioning for parts, at the same time critically scrutinizing each other like interviewers sizing up job applicants.

In the days and dates to come, we continue appraising, evaluating, and parleying with the tough practicality of merchants. But sooner or later—with love at first sight, first kiss, or first caress—pragmatic analysis fades away and cupidity takes it place. Emotions rush in and fantasy takes over, clouding our previous sound judgment. Each of us projects our preconceived dream on the stranger before us like a movie on a screen. We exaggerate qualities and dismiss defects, assembling near-perfect imaginary partners. Then we're thrilled to see our desires personified, our hopes incredibly fulfilled.

With love in bloom, I cuddle up to her winning image as she melts in my enamored gaze. The imprisoning walls of our former solitude burst like a dam. We gush forth our likes and dislikes, our hopes and dreams, and, more guardedly, our past and anticipated future. The sudden rush of intimacy feels wonderful. At last we've found someone who understands us and makes us feel wanted and needed!

I'm in love. My past loves seemed real at the time, but I know now they were not really love at all. This time, it's the real thing. And more than that, it's a special kind of love. No one ever has felt like this before. Thrills tickle the pit of my stomach. Pressure strains in my chest. The intensity of my feelings leaves me sure that this love is true, deep, and everlasting.

I want her. I need her. I can't bear to be without her. I think of her day and night. I slip into languorous dreams about her loveliness, heaving sighs of pleasure and fulfillment. I find it hard to concentrate or sleep. I don't feel like eating. I neglect important interests, put off obligations, disregard family and friends. My obsession with her might disrupt my life completely. But I don't care. I'm a slave of love, helpless in its bondage. I want to be with her always in eternal symbiosis, Siamese twins joined at the heart.

I haven't told her that I love her yet. I don't dare, because I'm not sure she feels the same about me. Premature disclosure of feelings can be risky, even ruinous. Yet I long for reciprocation of my feelings, which at this stage is more important than sex or any other fulfillment.

Finally we exchange the three little words—"I love you!"—and my heart, or ego, soars. I'm no longer insecure or inadequate—a self-estimate that some psychologists might say begins with a mother's failure to grant unconditional acceptance. Basking in the radiance of her love, I suddenly feel valuable, powerful, invincible.

I'm loved, loveable, and loving. I love life, the world, and everything in it. My whole existence is brighter, more vivid, and exciting. I dwell in endless springtime. Love is here to stay—and we've only just begun.

BYE BYE, LOVE

Our emotional high can last for weeks or months but rarely will it endure for years. As much as we might long to keep the thrills alive, time takes a toll on romantic fascination. Lovers grow discerning. Reality intrudes. Partners become critical. Dreamers demand that real people live up to their illusions. Love is blind, but only for a while.

Clues to true identity once unseen or brushed aside begin fall into place like pieces in a jigsaw puzzle. We might become unnerved by what we see, leading us to probe, scrutinize, even investigate. In sensitive matters, we would rather not question each other directly. That could invite deception. Instead we guess, assess, infer, deduce, ask friends, consult horoscopes, and spy.

At first I found my Special Person's aura of mystery spellbinding. Now it feels like a barrier concealing parts of herself and her past. I have reason to suspect she's not as wholesome as I thought. I don't like her friends very much. Her voice is too high. She wears too much makeup. Her mind is shallow. She has a sharp tongue.

She's discovered I'm a clerk and not a manager, that I grab fast food instead of dine on fine cuisine, that I drove a borrowed vehicle our first few dates rather than a sports car of my own. I don't dress fashionably, she says, and I don't keep my fingernails clean. My character, as she sees it now, inspires less than admiration.

As illusions turn to disillusion—an inevitable feature of modern romance—I begin to wonder if this love is really real or only infatuation. Is it true love or false, deep love or shallow, eternal love or passing fancy? Is it love at all or just a fixation, a compulsion, an obsession, an addiction, a fantasy, a crush, aim-inhibited sex, or just sex? Doubts nag me day and night. I'm disappointed, disenchanted, deceived, cheated, injured, betrayed. The feeling's gone and I just can't get it back.

I want to withdraw, though it's not time yet to break up. Romantic bonds are like an unspoken contract, and any breach must be justified with reasons. I start an argument. I try to catch her in a lie. I patrol her home late into the night, hoping to find her with another guy. I interrogate friends to gather incriminating evidence.

Ultimately romancers break off for all the reasons they can think of. Apparently this is nothing new. Some three thousand years ago the Hebrew King Solomon observed in a biblical proverb: "In estrangement one seeks pretexts; with all persistence he picks a quarrel."

Enough quarrels leave us both as free as birds. Yet neither of us feels happy. Where lovers used to croon "Love Me Forever," we plead "Help Me Make It Through the Night."

I'm desolate, with an aching in my chest, a hollowness in the pit of my stomach. My glorious dreams of love lie shattered in a thousand pieces. I dwell in a wintertime of loneliness. My life has little hope or meaning. My future seems empty and bleak. "She's gone . . . and my relief/ Must be to loath her," as Shakespeare's Othello describes my emotions about her now.

A first romance in ruins feels like the end of the world. But serial romancers know better. Experience has assured them that time heals, more or less. They know they will recover, as though from a sickness, slowly but steadily. And if, on the rebound, they find another Special Person to fill their aching hearts, they can bounce ahead into fresh romantic bliss at once.

For the meantime, however, they wrack their minds, trying to understand what went wrong. They did as they were told to do by magazines, pop songs, movies, and media advisers. They learned and absorbed their society's counsel and practiced it almost to the letter. Why, then, did love, which was supposed make their lives complete, fail them so completely?

Love Foredoomed

INCOMPLETE LOVE

WHAT'S WRONG with romance as our fable describes it? Primarily, as a way of loving, it is incomplete:

+ The romancers involved are not yet inwardly whole. They are too emotionally needy to be likely to love in a beneficial, giving way.
+ Their sense of self-worth is incomplete. They depend on others for personal validation.
+ They have not cultivated traits of character that lead to an ability to love effectively: honesty, openness, kindness, generosity, an attitude of service.
+ They lay the groundwork for incomplete acceptance when they conjure up a Special Person in advance, making a shopping list of specifications rather than preparing to meet and accept people as they are.
+ They make authentic relationships vastly incomplete by posing and posturing, and by holding excessive expectations, fantasies, and Pygmalion-like dreams of perfect partners.
+ Their incomplete authenticity dooms love to incompleteness. As philosophers and great saints have observed: We cannot love who we do not know.
+ A consumer-orientation, focused more on getting than giving, on

consuming than producing, assures an incomplete love where partners drain one another then must break apart to emotionally recover.

Looking Back in Anger

We all know how love relationships can devastate us personally when they turn dull and disappointing, painful and caustic, empty and unenduring. Ecstasies give way to brooding, jealousy, quarrels, separations, bittersweet reunions, rejections, departures, regrets, and remorse.

Many lovers who once filled each other's lives to overflowing are left raw with resentment at the end of their affairs. They deny one another common courtesies they would freely offer to strangers. They exchange no notes or telephone calls. They ignore special days that once demanded scrupulous attention. They dispose of mementos once held precious, discard gifts, destroy photographs. Dreams and memories once tenderly treasured they recall only with distaste. "Ex-lovers make great speed bumps!" declares a bumper sticker, attesting to love turned to bitter animosity. Former romancers commonly hope never to meet again.

Disenchanted lovers who have invested heavily in a failed relationship often look back in anger and ahead in fury. They have been known to soak an ex's clothes in bleach, scratch expensive cars, uncork costly wines, stuff curtain rails with rotting shrimp. They stalk, beat, knife, shoot, and send bombs to former intimates.

Injury and pain are virtually inescapable with our current incomplete style of love. We have come to accept the agony of broken hearts—in past times a major tragedy—as a mere developmental task for youth and a natural part of love ever after. Yet failed love remains one of life's most devastating experiences. As the nineteenth-century French novelist Honoré de Balzac observed, "There are no little events with the heart."

After a first breakup, teenage girls can be overwhelmed by a sense of loss and inadequacy, crying in solitude night after night and losing unhealthy amounts of weight. Shattered romance for anyone can lead to damaged confidence, loss of purpose, loneliness, depression, physical or mental illness, even suicide.

Though emotional pains often heal fairly well with time, a multitude of consequences, personal and social, stay with us to affect our lives. Falling in love then falling out again leaves our outlook on love, other people, and the course of our existence changed forever.

Lovers buffeted harshly and repeatedly by the miseries of failed romance can become poisoned with suspicion and fear of exploitation. Jolted from one rocky liaison to another, they come to dread the agonies of love. Some withdraw into "amorophobia," as one psychologist classified fear of falling in love and forming emotional commitments. For the severely disappointed, romance takes on the look of a dirty trick, a roller coaster ride to nowhere, selfish, callous, dangerous, deadly, a battlefield of strategies and tactics, a brothel of uncommitted sex, an emotional slaughterhouse.

INEFFECTIVE EXPERTS

An anthropologist studying the Hopi Indians once asked a tribesman why so many of their songs were about rain. The Hopi man answered, "Because rain is scarce." Then he asked, "Isn't that why so many of your songs are about love?"

Yet why should we modern people find love scarce? We think about love, talk about love, dream about love, read about love. Love waltzes, brawls, and swelters across our movie and television screens. Printing presses spill off pages by the millions exalting love, explaining love, analyzing love, celebrating love, dramatizing love, defaming love. If love leaves us perplexed and distraught, mass media advisors stand ready with witty answers to our most impassioned questions.

Such profound interest and involvement would make us experts in any other field. Why, then, are we not experts in love? Our failures seem to make no sense. Even professing Christians, with a religion of love that says God is love, have the same basic problems with love as the rest of the population.

We stumble through love as if we knew nothing. We search for it, sometimes with manic intensity, yearning, hoping, expecting lasting bliss. Yet all too often we end up frustrated and disillusioned.

A writer once observed that some people go thorough life wondering what hit them. Most of us go through love that way. This suggests that our problems with love are at least partly accidental.

When we choose to love, we do not also choose to fail. People who have suffered disappointing romances did not have that planned. Once their hopes were glowing. Casualties of divorce did not wish shattered marriage on themselves. Almost always they hoped for stability and happiness. Parents with children turning secretive, distrustful, arrogant, or hostile did not plan that for their families. They meant to create a home warm and rich in love. Miscarriages of love are nothing we design or anticipate.

So where does the failure lie?

Certainly not with love itself, as some disappointed lovers imagine. Love has no force or motion of its own. It does not exist as an independent thing. Rather, love is an activity, something people do. It succeeds or fails only because you and I succeed or fail in doing it.

When our experience of love falls short of our intentions, it is largely because we did not understand how to make our love succeed. No one has told us and we have not learned by ourselves.

I propose that our failures in love begin with the culture that teaches us to love. We are poorly instructed by what commonly is called a "sick society." Since the sickness in question most obviously is not physical nor intellectual but emotional, we are badly misled by its council in emotional matters.

If in matters of love we join the social milieu, by conscious choice or unconscious default, we condemn ourselves to faulty advice and a failed system of love. Then like everyone else we are sure to be left with incomplete love that promises one thing yet delivers another. If, on the other hand, we take a hard and critical look at what the society has taught us, we can begin to find our way to more complete, successful love.

Love Befuddled

WE HAVE BEEN POISONED BY FAIRY TALES.

—ANAIS NIN (1903–1977)

LESSONS IN LOVE

WHO TAUGHT US our oddly unsuccessful kind of love? Why, the princess and the frog, and a girl who lived with dwarfs, and a sooty young woman who lost a glass slipper that, as luck would have it, was found by a handsome prince. Our society is shot through with fables of romance that we absorb from earliest childhood.

Ordinarily the teaching process starts with the family. Often the lessons are vague. I grew up thinking of love mainly as a feeling, an emotion so internal that it might or might not affect anyone beyond the lover. This sort of love at times could beam forth warmly in fondness or affection, but it carried no guarantee of kindness and active care. All in all, love struck me as confusing, and sometimes self-contradictory.

All through my childhood and into advanced youth, I excluded the word "love" from my vocabulary. Having no clear notion what it meant, I found the term awkward and embarrassing. I also distrusted what passed for love in the society around us. Whatever it was, for all the trouble it caused, it didn't seem worthy of the name.

In church I heard a message about another kind of love that turned the other cheek when the first was slapped, gave the shirt off one's back, bestowed kindness upon enemies, and conferred generous gifts expecting nothing in return. I found that idea appealing. Yet I could not think of anyone I knew who dared to behave that way. So like almost everyone, I fell back on the society at large for instructions on love.

Anthropologist Margaret Mead, writing in *Life* magazine, observed that people growing up in the 1960s were "the first generation who have been brought up by the media instead of by parents." Actually, the mass media took control over love even before that. Movies and the press were telling people what to do about love as early as the 1920s. Today the media's influence is all-pervasive, greater than the family's, mightier than God's, teaching us most of what we think we understand about love.

And we tend to accept what the media says, no matter what it says. We devour a vast literature of books and articles on love. We seek the counsel of media gurus who purport to solve love's riddles. An Internet search for "relationship advice" offers almost six million sites. We watch love lessons on stage and screen. Meanwhile, love ballads croon a background theme for our lives; by one count, eighty-five percent of popular songs lilt and lament about romance.

Yet who creates these books and articles? Who dispenses the advice? Who makes the movies? Who spins out the songs? Some of the sources are certified "experts"—modern shamans of the heart. Many others may or may not hold special knowledge, wisdom, or experience.

Is the media really competent for this critical task? Do the lives of its love-guides demonstrate their fitness to teach us? Are their characters lofty, their marriages sublime, their children exemplary? In most cases, we don't know. The social authority is largely anonymous, as unaccountable for what it says as it is often irresponsible for saying anything at all. In the few cases where we do know something of the source, the knowledge is not always encouraging.

But the media cares as little about real competence as it does about the welfare of readers, viewers, and listeners. Its mission is commerce— to exploit the libido for profit.

Meanwhile, the deluge of advice, information, and delusions—most of it muggy-minded and misleading—works like propaganda on our thoughts and hearts. It weaves lavish illusions, sumptuous dreams, absurdly inflated expectations. Yet all too often, as consumers of its counsel, we find the most important relationships of our lives seriously flawed if not in hopeless disarray.

The solution to our dilemma obviously is not to go back to the media for more of its advice. Yet what alternatives do we have? Very few. Unlike ancient philosophies of East and West, the historic Christian church, and other major religious traditions, our society offers little profound literature on love and less serious teaching. We are left only to think for ourselves and blaze a fresh trail through the wilderness of modern love.

Yet this trailblazing course seems so difficult and tricky that most of us simply go with the general flow. We take our lessons in love from the emotionally "sick society," soaking up what it says, whatever it says, then suffering the woeful consequences of conforming to its ways.

WHAT IS THIS THING?

"What is this thing called love?" asked a Cole Porter song in 1929. Now, several generations and multimillion media outpourings later, our society still is asking the same question, still puzzled, still without an answer.

How come? Haven't we learned anything about love since 1929? Worse, does the fateful question have no answer? Must we founder in despair through ruinous romances, maiming marriages, and fractured lives because all these things depend profoundly upon love—and there's no hope of understanding what love is, much less how to do it effectively?

But no, it's not that bad. A thing called love is there—genuinely true and beneficent love available to all of us. It is merely misplaced in a society that has lost love's meaning.

Shortly before Julius Caesar's day, ancient Rome's most prolific author, Marcus Varro, tallied 280 different opinions about the meaning of "good." With such vague guidelines, how could anybody find and do good? In our time, the word "love" is almost as confusing. Modern dictionaries offer some two dozen definitions. A thesaurus will suggest several hundred matches. The mass media deals with an infinity of different "loves."

Is love a sentiment, an attitude, a thrill, an emotion, a desire, a craving, an obsession, a weakness, a strength, a force, a passion, a madness, a physical urge, a divine benefaction, a way of life, a sampling of heaven, a preview of hell?

And how do we distinguish loving from liking, caring, affection, concern, attraction, infatuation, fixation, obsession? The word can signify respect, admiration, idolatry, possessiveness, dependence, sadism, and masochism.

People talk of love for self, friends, women or men, for all humankind; for principles, honor, virtue, and causes; for work and money, art and ideas, home and country, adventure and security, domesticity and travel; for meat, wine, chocolate, and love itself. They say they love God, parents, and pickles; children, movies, and cars; bicycling, skating, skiing, and sailing; sardines, popcorn, pop rock, and Bach. Lovers speak of falling in love, being in love, making love, and loving—all possibly suggesting different things. As English author Aldous Huxley wrote with the vehemence of a dedicated linguist, "Of all the worn, smudged, dogeared words in our vocabulary 'love' is surely the grubbiest, smelliest, slimiest. . . ."

"Let me love you tonight!" the seductive lover croons to his latest lady love, who loved their candlelight dinner and their talk of loving Paris but fears if they made love he might not love her in the morning.

"If you loved me you'd do this-or-that," urges the emotional extortionist.

"Love one another. . . ." says Jesus Christ. How's that again? We can be confident that Jesus and a multitude of saints from all the world's great religions knew exactly what they meant when they held forth love as humanity's highest endeavor. But in present-day language and with modern modes of thinking, how can we be sure of catching their meaning?

"Love" is one of the most ambiguous words in the English language. It can be used to describe almost any feeling but disgust—including hate, as in love-hate relationships. It also can be used to justify almost any action.

Researcher William Kephart asked university students, "Do you feel that you know what love really is?" Seventy-five percent of the males were not sure. Sixty-four percent of the females were uncertain.

Sociologist John Lee asked people from Britain, Canada, and the United States what love meant to them. He classified at least six distinct answers. Some of his subjects said love is romance played as a trifling game. Others described chaotic emotion, loss of appetite, sleeplessness. Some talked of merging with another person as a means of completing themselves. Others spoke of serene, stable, sweet affection and companionship. Some talked of sensible, practical relationships. Others cited altruistic love as preached by great religions, with its patience, kindness, and seeking after nothing in return. Many meant a mix of these interpretations.

The only consistent ingredient in all the things called love is a strong propensity *toward* something, whether self-oriented craving at one pole or selfless benevolence at the other. Between those extremes, the words "I love you" carry hardly more sure meaning than the message in an alphabet soup.

When words lose clarity, actions lose their true proportions. Even people who mean to love, not knowing what love means, cannot do it effectively. It seems no surprise, then, that with love lost in confusion, we also have lost effective love in our society and our lives.

Is Romance Universal?

The worst thing we are taught—by far the most misleading—is that modern-style romance is synonymous with love, that the two are identical. Our choice, then, is that or nothing. It becomes the only game in town, the only one worthwhile, perhaps the only kind of love that's ever been.

It isn't, of course. Romance is only one variety of love. And even romance has worn different faces through 2,500 years of Western history.

In some parts of the world, romance does not exist at all. Once I visited Tahiti as an unpaid deckhand aboard a small Norwegian cargo ship. This was before the fabled island opened up to mass tourism—"*la grande spoliation*," local people were lamenting—and before surviving remnants of the French Foreign Legion were based there. With relatively few visitors, Tahiti's local custom allowed a young woman to bed down with any man who caught her fancy. "What a deal!" many a foreign man thought, at least until he waxed romantic. If he then confessed dreamy feelings to his island love, he found she did not know what he was talking about. More generally, romantic love in social groups that make sex freely available rarely occurs in individuals and probably never as a social institution.

Other societies flatly reject romance. Bedouin peoples of North Africa and the Middle East regard romantic love as disgraceful; their marriages are made by families. Traditional Chinese society deemed romance dangerous; marriages were arranged by families or match-makers. Confucianism declared romantic love an unworthy sentiment linked to low moral standards and social disorder. Equally, all the world's great civilizations in most periods of their history have considered romance an inferior kind of love.

Among Australian aborigines, a girl who paired off to satisfy romantic desires was judged little different from a prostitute. Disapproval of romantic love also has prevailed in many of the other cultures we call "primitive."

In some societies romantic unions were illegal. In Korea until 1910, marriage based on romance was deemed illegitimate and was subject to severe punishment.

All this is not to imply that the practice of romantic love is unique to modern Western culture. In 1992, anthropologists William Jankowiak of the University of Nevada-Las Vegas and Edward Fischer of Tulane University in New Orleans studied 168 widely varying societies and found some evidence of romantic love in at least 147 of them. A product of human emotion rather than an intellectual invention, romance turns up in literature and legend around the world. Folk tales usually describe it in terms of ecstasy or anguish or both. More often than not, romancers meet disaster, except in children's tales where lovers wed and live happily ever after.

Yet rarely in any place or time has romance been accepted as a sound and healthy activity for real life. Generally it has been censured as a menace to marriage, family, future offspring, and orderly society. And for good reason: As social psychologist David G. Myers cites, "As it happens, what the heart says is a notoriously fragile foundation for long-term marital success. . . ." and ". . . cultures that base marriage on romantic love have the highest divorce rates."

It should come as no surprise, then, that love—equated with romance—is so befuddled in our time. Romance, unrestrained or even controlled, always has been befuddling. Yet the confusion we suffer probably is worse than it has been for two thousand years. For all our preoccupation with love and our eager efforts to find it, we end up more pained and frustrated by love than anyone since the people of ancient Rome, who lent romance its name.

Love in History

LOVE AMONG THE ANCIENTS

THE SONG OF SONGS in the Bible's Old Testament, attributed to King Solomon of the tenth century BC, celebrates tender romance in lyrical terms. Its verses, referring to "my promised bride," make clear that the couple is engaged to be wed. The lovers' praises for each other resemble love songs of ancient Egypt. First-century Jews used the Song of Songs at marriage feasts.

Such sentiments have echoed happily through the ages whenever young men and women felt agreeably matched for betrothal or wedlock. Yet rarely has history looked kindly on romance as the main foundation for marriage or a license for unwed passions.

Egyptian hieroglyphic poems describe passion-love as all-consuming and obsessive, resembling insanity, a shameful weakness to be hidden from others. Very ancient Greeks and early Romans had little or nothing to do with romantic love. Yet they were aware of its fervors. As early as the sixth century BC, the female lyric poet Sappho from the Greek island of Lesbos recorded its symptoms: emotional agitation, loss of appetite, sleeplessness, fever, heartache.

In ancient Sparta, young men whose families had not arranged marriages for them were pushed into a dark chamber with an equal number of young women to grope for their lifetime mates. Spartans believed this method of pairing husbands and wives was no blinder than erotic love. For them love was best when it came after marriage rather than before. Meanwhile, marital affection in Sparta appears to have been as strong as in any other civilized culture. Spartans boasted of having no adultery among them and divorce was rare.

Generally in history, romance flourishes at times of relative wealth. An emotional luxury, it requires full stomachs and some degree of leisure to thrive. As the English clergyman and scholar Robert Burton pointed out in 1621 in *The Anatomy of Melancholy*, love grows cold when food and drink become scarce.

History also shows that societies laying heavy emphasis on sex— which tends to go along with romance—lack a sense of social purpose. Seeing no more worlds to conquer, they pursue comfort and pleasure, which leads to a self-seeking form of love rather than more altruistic kinds. So it was in Imperial Rome, in India during the Gupta Dynasty of the fourth to sixth centuries, in China during the T'ang Dynasty of the seventh to tenth centuries, in seventeenth-century France of Louis XIV, and in modern society beginning with Victorian England.

Ancient Greeks later in their history practiced sentimental love as a sensuous amusement with boys and prostitutes, though not as a prelude to marriage. In Athens, writes the classical scholar and archaeologist Karl Otfried Müller, "we have not a single instance of a man having loved a free-born woman, and marrying her from affection." Some Greeks praised sentimental love, especially man-boy infatuations, though where sex was preeminent the boys often complained of being exploited. Other Greeks called romantic love *theia mania*, or madness from the gods, understanding their gods to be more capricious than beneficent.

In ancient Rome marriage was essentially a family contract. By the time of Julius Caesar, however, Romans also were pursuing romance as a voluptuous game. Their pastime inspired the word "romance" itself. The Latin *romanice* means "in the Roman manner." In later French it became *roman* or *romanz*. The English of the Middle Ages rendered the word "*romauns*" or "*romaunce*," which in time became "romance."

Romans carried on love affairs mainly for raw sensations. Their romantic romps seethed with sensuality, ecstasy, quarreling, obscenity, and mutual torment. A typical lover stayed with a partner until bored or weary then went off to a new affair, much as people commonly do today. Adultery was popular, savored as a sporting adventure.

Odi et amo—I hate and I love! Thus did Gaius Valerius Catullus, Rome's greatest lyric poet, write about the beautiful wife of a provincial governor whom he adored with frenzied passion. A liberated woman of her time, she dallied with men freely, much to Catullus's dismay. Yet he continued to love her tormentedly, even as she degenerated into a drunken slattern roaming the streets in search of sexual liaisons with strangers. His romance was more or less typical of the period.

Meanwhile, men increasingly remained single, marriages diminished infertility, and divorce became easy and informal for both men and women. By the time of Christ, the Roman birthrate had plunged so drastically that the Emperor Augustus Caesar passed desperate legislation supporting morals and the family. But neither laws nor anything else worked. Though the empire was highly developed, well organized, well ruled, rich, and peaceful, by the end of the second century it was so depleted of population that anyone in Italy or the provinces could freely occupy untenanted land and gain full title merely by bringing it under cultivation.

The disintegration of family life led to widespread emotional frustration and loneliness. Meanwhile, the feverish eroticism was burning itself out in excesses and over-refinement, leaving only jaded appetites, weariness, and boredom.

The Roman Empire's sensuous taste in love evoked some social backlash. The first-century BC Epicurean poet-philosopher Lucretius warned against passion-love, calling it destructive madness. Some Romans decried sensuous love as a consequence of faulty character and a menace to individuals and society at large. Lucretius, who saw sexualized romance as a trap and a disease as well as a delusion, advised in the poem *De Rerum Natura* that sensual passion be avoided as habit-forming, inducing frenzy, causing irrational behavior, consuming strength, and squandering life's substance.

First-century philosopher Musonius Rufus spoke against sexual acts outside marriage, while Stoics and Neoplatonists maintained rigorous self-control in this and other areas of life. The Roman poet Ovid, who portrayed the lover as a trembling, pale, sighing, sleepless slave of passion who could even die of the malady, recommended a way to become love-proof: "Love yields to business," he advised. "Be employed and you're safe."

Roman moralists cited romance and its consequences as a significant cause of the empire's social ills. Many modern historians agree that the style of love helped undermine the once-robust Roman character and more generally is a symptom of a culture on the wane.

Early Christians joined the reaction against supersensual Roman love. Admonishing against not only unrestrained romance but seeking after pleasures of the senses in general, they urged control of carnal appetites: "For the desires of the flesh are against the Spirit, and the desires of the Spirit are against the flesh," taught the Apostle Paul to converts of Galatia in Asia Minor. "And those who belong to Christ Jesus have crucified the flesh with its passions and desires" (Galatians 5:17, 24). As Christianity took hold in the ancient world, love in the Roman manner came to an end.

LOVE IN THE MIDDLE AGES

"Out of love, place yourselves at one another's service," the Apostle Paul also preached, echoing the Christian ideal of love as active goodwill. Many people seeking the way of Christ-love did just that for hundreds of years. Meanwhile, love as emotional passion outside marriage was condemned as a danger to life, the soul, and eternal salvation.

As barbarians warred and the church taught altruism, romance lay dormant until the end of the eleventh century. When it reappeared, it took a wholly new form. Just as romance is only one variety of love, so do variations arise within romance itself.

Poets and noblemen in southern France revived romance as *l'amour courtois*, or courtly love. The trend began with a treatise titled *The Art of Courtly Love*. Its author, a churchman named Andreas Capellanus, first described his topic then denounced it, testifying, "from Scripture we know that the Devil is really the author of [romantic] love and lechery."

About the same time, *Tristan and Isolde* gave fictional flesh to the new idea. The earliest known tale of romance in modern Western tradition, the story tells about a young knight Tristan from England who travels to Ireland on a mission to bring back the beautiful Queen Isolde as the bride for his uncle, King Mark. Along their journey the couple unwittingly share a magical love potion that brings hearts into rapturous union for about three years. The tale ends with the death of both lovers.

Courtly love appealed to feudal nobles with wealth and leisure. At first it was only a literary fad. Troubadours of southern France and upper Italy, *trouveres* of northern France, and *minnesingers* from German lands traveled through Europe singing narratives of love and valiant deeds. A kind of medieval soap opera, the performances were enormously popular. Today, despite the loss of much literature of the time, we still know the names of 460 of the poet-musicians and have on record 2,500 of their works.

The fanciful ideal of courtly love gradually evolved into a serious social philosophy. Daydreams of romance led to actions. At first gallant swains and noble ladies practiced exercises in ardor and adulation playfully. But soon they were pursuing *l'amour courtois* with fervor. The remnants of their pastime can be seen in love's manners and morals to this day.

Courtly love bore little similarity to romance as known and done by either ancient Romans or present-day people. Extolled as the noblest emotion the human heart could cultivate, it brought knights and squires into faithful allegiance to beautiful, highborn women. The relationships resembled the link between vassal and lord. The chivalrous servants of love fought in tournaments, embarked on dangerous quests, and ventured forth on crusades, dedicating their trials to their special ladies, seeking honor and happiness solely through hardship and devotion. Their love was intended to be spiritually uplifting, transfiguring their souls by tempering them into finer men and stronger warriors.

Though some courtly affairs ended with "agreeable and sweet sport" in the lady's bedchamber, most remained scrupulously chaste. Dashing knights saw their fair damsels as untouchable icons to be adored from afar. Some lovers referred to their ladies as "Madonna," or the mother of Christ.

"Nor kiss I ask, nor sweet embraces, lest I were blaspheming," the troubadour Gaucelm Faidit sang. A noble lover usually sought no more than the pleasure of adoring the beauty and grace of his mistress—if granted the privilege of seeing her at all, since she could be the protected wife of a powerful ruler or a sheltered daughter.

Marriage was out of the question in courtly love. A twelfth-century arbiter of romance, Countess Marie of Champagne, proclaimed: "We declare and we hold as firmly established that love cannot exert its powers between two people who are married to each other. For lovers give each other everything freely, under no compulsion of necessity, but married people are in duty bound to give in to each other's desires and deny themselves to each other in nothing." A thirteenth-century Countess of Narbonne agreed, insisting that, "Conjugal affection has absolutely nothing in common with love. We say 'absolutely,' and with all consideration, that love cannot exist between husband and wife."

Thus did love in the courtly manner remain a bittersweet yearning unfulfilled. It was an odd mix of idealistic romance and religious altruism: ardent longing after an image of perfection, and pure service never seeking a return. Always difficult, endlessly frustrating, refining the spirit with struggle and privation, it was the tender emotion of mortal creatures who strove to rise to immortal heights.

It also was regarded by many as somewhat inane. "Love is a folly of the mind, an unquenchable fire, a hunger without surfeit, a sweet delight, a pleasing madness, a labor without repose and a repose without labor," wrote Richard de Fournival in the thirteenth century. The church went further in negative judgment, branding courtly love a heresy and linking it with idolatry and an unhealthy yearning for sorrow and death.

Yet even as medieval times moved toward the Renaissance, the habits and sentiments of courtly love persisted. The thirteenth-century Italian poet Dante Alighieri first laid eyes on his beloved Beatrice when he was nine years old, then worshipped her for years with a pure, inspiring love. Yet he rarely saw her, never met her in person, and never spoke a single word to her. Dante also agreed with detractors of romance that this kind of love was accompanied by a flight from reason.

The fourteenth-century poet Petrarch had a long-distance relationship with a lady he called Laura. His sonnets about her were read and emulated for centuries. Meanwhile, the real woman behind his verses was stalwartly bearing eleven children to her husband. Countless lovers thereafter admired ladies from afar, wrote poems to them, prayed for meager favors, sighed with privation, and wept in delicious despair.

Meanwhile, marriage remained separate from romantic love, a practical institution. Among the lower classes, wedlock built households and cared for family welfare. For the wealthy, it also served political and economic ends. A leading educator of the sixteenth century, Juan Luis Vives, advised, "I would not counsel ye to marry her with whom thou hast been in amours withal." Alessandro Piccolomini, an Italian of the same period, explained why: "Love is a reciprocity of soul and has a different end and obeys different laws from marriage."

ENLIGHTENMENT LOVES

Twenty years after Piccolomini separated love and marriage, he yielded to changing social attitudes and brought the two together. He granted that loving feelings were good and proper on the pathway to marriage and along the road of wedded life.

By the seventeenth century, Daniel Rogers, a staunch British Puritan, wrote in a book titled *Matrimonial Life*, "Husbands and wives should be as two sweet friends, bred under one constellation, tempered by an influence from heaven, whereof neither can give any great reason save that mercy and providence first made them so, and then made their match." The Puritan English poet John Milton agreed, deeming wedded love one of life's greatest fulfillments. So did William Penn, founder of the Pennsylvania Quaker colony, who advised simply, "Never marry but for love."

The leading intellectual current of the period, however, counseled differently. The seventeenth- and eighteenth-centuries' Age of Enlightenment valued cool reason over emotion. Romantic love was mere superstition belonging to humankind's immature past. Urbane self-control rather than enslavement to feelings was the order of the day.

And how was romance to be practiced? As no more than sensuality, an intricate pastime of flirtation, seduction, and adultery. "There is nothing good in love but the physical part," the Comte de Buffon, a scientific naturalist, advised.

The French aristocrat and moralist La Rochefoucauld thought even less of romance. "If love is judged by most of its effects," he wrote, "it resembles hate more than friendship." He also believed that, "people would never fall in love if they had not heard love talked about."

Yet as time went by, the sweeter view of Puritans and Quakers won out. With the birth and growth of the Industrial Age, the focus of life moved from countryside to towns. There the tastes and customs of landowning aristocrats ceased to be the ruling mode. A newly prospering middle class set trends that would dominate the way people love to the present day.

ROMANCE REVIVED

Jean Jacques Rousseau had a lot to do with the revival of romantic love. The Swiss-born eighteenth-century social philosopher, political theorist, novelist, playwright, and opera composer gave expression to a fresh set of romantic ideals.

Rousseau's personal love life was odd, to say the least. He candidly declared sexual intercourse to be the greatest of life's pleasures. Yet he did not enjoy it as often as he might have liked. He learned the art at the age of twenty-one with a young widow who had given him a home since he was sixteen, and whom he called "Mama." He later wrote, "To fall on my knees before a masterful mistress, to obey her commands, to beg her forgiveness, have been to me the most delicate of pleasures." Yet, he found, "This way of making love does not lead to rapid progress." Consequently he possessed few women.

Meanwhile, in his literary role as worshipper of nature, political liberal, and shaper of nineteenth-century romanticism, Rousseau wrote novels of pure and perfect love. He idealized womanhood as demure and delicate, sweet and tender, modest and pure. True love, he asserted, was single-hearted, with but one ideal match for each earthly soul.

Love lost was a tragedy. Love found promised devoted and tranquil family life.

The French savored his ideals. So did contemporary Germans. The conservative British statesman Edmund Burke, on the other hand, branded Rousseau's teaching a sexual revolution aligned with the political revolutions of the age: "a love without gallantry," he huffed, ". . . indelicate, sour, gloomy, ferocious. . . ." But no matter. Most English people liked it, too. Thus the pattern for love was set for the Victorian age.

VICTORIAN LOVE

Much of Victorian culture represents a desperate clinging to things passing away, a rearguard defense, a last-ditch stand. Against what? Crumbling cultural mores, an anthropologist might say. The disintegration of Western civilization, according to German philosopher Oswald Spengler, English historian Arnold Toynbee, and Harvard sociologist Pitirim Sorokin. Whatever Victorians were conserving so tenaciously, their society practiced exaggerated manners and morals, customs and views to the point of parody.

In an effort to resurrect medieval courtly love, Victorians took an opposite course from their forebears in the Age of Reason. While Enlightenment people bridled their emotions but let sexuality romp freely, Victorians rejected sex almost altogether, at least philosophically. They pushed sexual feelings out of consciousness as unworthy of their dignity, repressing their urges, as psychoanalyst Sigmund Freud put it, sometimes to the point of neurosis. At the same time they unleashed emotions to rollick like nature in the wild. Like Rousseau, they accepted that human beings and their instincts, but for the corrupting influences of civilization, were naturally good.

The English public perused *Sentimental Magazine* while the poet John Keats wrote an ode to melancholy. Lord Byron penned romantic poems and pursued love affairs as he dragged his bleeding, manic-depressive heart across Europe. Ministers of religion wept at the altar. Brides fainted. A young student separated from his ladylove for several weeks told her in a letter that his sadness moved him to bellow through a forest like a demon, writhing on the ground, grinding branches in his teeth, and finally biting off a piece of one hand and spitting it out in frenzy. All this, among Victorian romantics, was admired.

As in medieval times, maidens were celebrated for grace, delicacy, and purity. Unlike days of yore, however, love and marriage went together like a horse and carriage. The home was idealized as a man's castle, a woman's haven, a child's nurturing nest. Fathers ventured out to brave the ruthless challenges of *laissez-faire* capitalism, then returned to the civilizing influences of a woman's love. As the English poet Robert Browning wrote to his future wife, Elizabeth Barrett, "Give me your counsel at all times, beloved: I am wholly open to your desires, and teaching, and direction. Try what you can make of me."

Meanwhile, nineteenth-century couples gained the right to marry, with parental consent, as a union of individuals rather than of lineages, for companionship instead of economic or political expediency.

Romance in Flames

Theodore Roosevelt—rough-riding soldier, bully president, big-game hunter, and Amazon explorer—talked as a young man of keeping himself "pure" for some "rare and radiant maiden." Yet long before he died in 1919, the dean of women at Northwestern University told coeds in chapel, "I have heard . . . that some young women allow men to touch them, to hold their hands. . . ." and a distinguished speaker at a women's college graduation warned parents of the ease with which young ladies were allowing themselves to be kissed. Meanwhile, the ideal of love as willing giving of self was waning, replaced first by an austere sense of duty then by self-preoccupied wanting and needing. Times, people, and love were changing again.

The cataclysm of World War I speeded social transformation, as major wars always do. The war brought down empires, shook civilization, led to the collapse of the brittle bastions of Victorian morality, and thoroughly disoriented the young.

The Lost Generation of the Jazz Age danced onto the scene as stylish pleasure-seekers. Elders stood aghast at their hip-flasks, slangy speech, and casual parties. Erotic fashions in dress, literature, and motion pictures filled young minds with sensual ideas. The advent of the automobile made the emotional and physical titillations of "sparking" and "pitching woo" readily attainable.

In the social revolution of the 1920s, Flaming Youth invented dating, the most significant revolution in courtship for centuries. Before then, when a young swain spied a demure maiden, she would blush and cast her eyes downward. He would ask her father if he might come calling. If that were permitted, the couple would spend an afternoon in her parlor playing the piano or reading poetry while an aunt crocheted in a corner as chaperon. This was followed by "walking out" and "keeping company," a one-and-only relationship expected to end in wedlock.

Dating, on the other hand, implied no commitment at all. It offered romance as breezy entertainment. People met informally, made carefree dates, then sallied off in cars to spend evenings at movies, in speakeasies, and parked on back roads. Parents were shocked to hear of a new practice among the young called "necking."

Rapid urbanization, disillusion with authority, and easy affluence helped loosen traditional morals all the more. So did Freud's dire warnings about the effects of repressed sexual desire, which made erotic freedom appear more or less scientifically approved.

By 1926, the social novelist F. Scott Fitzgerald complained that "the universal preoccupation with sex had become a nuisance." The divorce rate soared and, according to one estimate, as many as one million illegal abortions took place each year during the Roaring Twenties.

With dating accepted as a normal social pattern, American children hardly past puberty were thrust by eager mothers into dancing classes and juvenile parties. Soon afterward the children were left on their own in penny dances, sock hops, movie theater balconies, proms, and the ubiquitous automobile.

Most people by their late teens had experienced puppy love and crushes. Most also acquired skills in necking, many venturing on to "petting" while some were "going steady" and others "going all the way."

The gradual disintegration of traditional sexual morals over the decades of the twentieth century was not so much approved by the society as veiled by denial or accepted with a grudging shrug by elders who felt helpless to do anything about it. Church leaders and church members were divided in their response, some opposing the rampant sexuality, others accommodating themselves to the social trend to varying degrees.

In 1940 a public opinion poll found that the average American believed women kissed and petted too much before marriage. By the 1950s, nubile females were teetering on a tightrope between traditional virginity and sexual liberality, giving the impression of one or the other, as each current boyfriend seemed to desire.

The 1960s brought another sexual revolution, perhaps less a major change in habits than a rebellion against widespread sexual hypocrisy and an acceptance of liberal behavior already underway. Also in the 1960s, dating as a social system began to wane. In its place grew a blend of hanging out, random sex, and vague "relationships," all lacking the forms and protection of rules and etiquette, confusing, unpredictable.

Presently, it seems that romance has ripened to the point of decay. As liaisons run a typical course from sweet to sour to bitter, one-and-only loves are all but extinct while happily-ever-after romance has almost vanished except as a wistful daydream. In their place we find a mode of love that leaves almost everyone disappointed: multi-partnered, non-chivalrous, ungallant, un-idealistic, non-spiritual, hotly sexual, cool-hearted.

As in ancient Roman times, romantic love shows clear signs of losing social favor, hurried along by widespread divorce and virulent sexual diseases. A 2004 presidential plan to spend $1.5 billion to promote marriage seems reminiscent of the Emperor Augustus Caesar's sadly futile legislation supporting morals and family in declining Rome.

Meanwhile, today's youth are abandoned to confusion. Impaled on Cupid's arrow, they make and unmake love, not yet understanding that a better, fuller, lasting, and secure way of love can be achieved by anyone who seeks it.

Love among the Scientists

LOVE IS A VERY ELUSIVE ENTITY.
—SUSAN S. AND CLYDE HENDRICK

SCIENTISTS, though the leading gurus of our time, cannot reach agreement about the meaning and proper methodology of love. In a professional sense, they really don't like love very much. How, after all, can they measure it, count it, quantify it? How can they even define it? As love researchers Ellen Berscheid and Elaine Hatfield have pointed out, how can they come up with scientific experiments to assess dating, courtship, and marriage? Love often seems too nebulous for science to study seriously.

In the 1980s I attended a weekend conference on love at a major university. The large, informal gathering brought together academics and interested laymen alike. I don't recall a single clear conclusion emerging from the sessions. Yet the company was pleasant and interesting, and they sought understandings, a bold step in itself in a professional climate often unfriendly to the topic.

The United States government gave it a few tries as well. In one instance in 1975, the National Science Foundation was spending $83,000 of federal funds in an effort to discover why people fall in love. They hoped to find clues that would help explain rising divorce rates and declining trust in family living as the basis for American life. The results were not momentous.

Empirical research into love probably began in the 1970s with social psychologist Zick Rubin, who developed psychometrically sound scales for measuring liking and loving. Since then, in a gradual way, the academic field of study often called "close-relationships research" has emerged among psychologists and sociologists. Also participating are scholars of other disciplines, such as communications, family studies, human development, and nursing. Rounding out the group are philosophers, theologians, and journalists. As promising as this surge of cross-disciplinary interest might seem, major conclusions are still pending.

Close-relationships researchers Susan and Clyde Hendrick of Texas Tech University confess in their book *Romantic Love,* "Perhaps the clearest finding from the current research on love and related variables is that our theoretical and empirical answers to the question 'What is love?' have really raised more questions." They also point out, "The scientific study of love is really just beginning."

Science in the Dark

Social scientists long have admitted to gaping holes in their knowledge of love. The Swiss psychiatrist Carl Gustav Jung proclaimed the problem of love "one of immense scope and intricacy." He assumed it always would remain open to question. Abraham Maslow, one of the founders of the humanistic psychology movement, remarked in 1954, "It is amazing how little the empirical sciences have to offer on the subject of love."

When Dorothy Tennov, a behaviorist psychologist, researched textbooks in her field in the 1960s as she worked on her excellent book, *Love and Limerence,* she found no reference to romantic, passionate, or erotic love. "In many books," she testified, "'love' was not even listed."

More than three decades later, medical doctor Dean Ornish wrote in his book *Love and Survival,* "You might think that *love* would be in the domain of psychologists, yet a review of the *Annual Review of Psychology* (twenty-three volumes!) found not a single reference to love." Adds professor of psychiatry James J. Lynch of the University of Maryland, "love is certainly a word that is taboo in science."

Citing the professional silence surrounding the study and analysis of love, Tennov observed, "No one feels entirely comfortable with the subject." When she delivered a paper on romantic love at an annual convention of the American Psychological Association, one man in the audience objected to her treating the topic in a scientific manner. A young woman there told Tennov that her own proposal of love as a subject for a doctoral dissertation had been rejected.

Yet, as Harvard sociologist Pitirim Sorokin observed, while many social scientists "quite illogically stigmatized as theological preaching or non-scientific speculation any investigation of the phenomena of love," at the same time they "viewed the phenomena of hatred, crime, war, and mental disorders as legitimate objects for scientific study. . . ."

The Austrian psychologist Theodor Reik explained this love-shy attitude as early as 1941. "Psychologists discuss sex very fully nowadays," he wrote, "but there is a conspiracy of silence about love. They avoid the subject, they seem to be embarrassed whenever it is mentioned." He added, "If they keep us in the dark about the genesis and character of love, it must be because they are in the dark themselves."

Only since the late twentieth century have scientists shown a change of heart about love, studying it across a broad range of disciplines from social to chemical. So far, however, poets, philosophers, and storytellers do a better job explaining love than scientists with their rigorous empirical methods.

SCIENCE LOOKS FOR LOVE

The Austrian doctor Sigmund Freud, who founded psychoanalysis early in the twentieth century, pioneered the clinical study of love. He believed that human love derives from sexual desire. Tender feelings, affection, friendship, and other nonsexual expressions of love he equally attributed to sex, branding them "aim-inhibited sexuality." Freud saw love as acquisitive in origin, yet he also made room for benevolent desires, declaring them the essential ingredient in "real, true, actual love." Even that, however, he saw as aim-inhibited sex.

Along with his libidinous interpretation of love, Freud also held a second concept: a cosmic view of love that encompasses all living things. He wrote of *eros*, in its classical meaning rather than its current sense, as the instinct that creates, unites, and renews every aspect of life against *thanatos*, or the death instinct. Ultimately, though, Freud admitted to insufficient understanding. Writing in a French magazine, he concluded, "Up to the present I have not found the courage to make any broad statements on the existence of love and I think that our knowledge is not sufficient to do so."

Karl Menninger, a Freudian disciple, who with his father, Charles, and his brother, William, founded the famed Menninger psychiatric clinic in Topeka, Kansas, built upon Freud's theory of love and death. In an age of annihilative wars, he was especially concerned about how love might overcome, absorb, or neutralize hate—the death instinct—in human beings.

While these and other thinkers probed love at its more profound levels, most social scientists tend to keep their musings on a romantic plane. William J. Goode contributed a definition of love to a 1959 issue of the *American Sociological Review:* "A strong emotional attachment, a cathexis, between adolescents or adults of opposite sexes, with at least the components of sex desire and tenderness." The pioneer English sexologist Havelock Ellis offered a simpler formula: Love = sex + friendship.

Theodor Reik, one of Freud's earliest and most brilliant pupils, departed from his mentor, seeing sex and love as altogether disparate things. Sex is an instinct, but romantic love is not, the Austrian psychologist asserted in his book *Of Love and Lust.* "The sex urge hunts for lustful pleasure; love is in search of joy and happiness."

Though sex and love can blend like coffee and cream, "Love is not originated in the sexual urge but belongs to the realm of the ego-drives," according to Reik. Each person conjures up a model self-image, an "ego-ideal," a portrait of personal perfection. Most people fall short of their own ideal, thus suffering a sense of inadequacy. When they meet someone who seems to have what they lack, they fall in love as a means of fulfilling their desired selves. "Two people who love each other are interchanging their ego-ideals," Reik wrote. "That they love each other means they love the ideal of themselves in the other one. There would be no love on earth if this phantom were not there."

When people are most unhappy with themselves and their lives, they are most vulnerable to romantic love, Reik claimed. Thus, "love does not spring from abundance and richness of the ego, but is a way out of inner distress and poverty." Likewise, people who feel satisfied with themselves find romantic love impossible.

Regrettably, Reik observed, "The love object is also a phantom to a great extent, a peg on which we hang all the illusions of ourselves which we longed to fulfill. The living person is, so to speak, only the material from which we create a fantastic figure, just as a sculptor shapes a statue out of stone." In time, reality catches up with most lovers. "Thus the falling out of love really means falling out of a dream, the daydream of a better self. . . . The liquidation leaves the ego in utter despair and misery."

Yet Reik wasn't quite finished with his appraisal of romance. Though he called romance "love" throughout his book in the popular manner of speaking, he concluded with a measure of confusion. "Romance is not identical with love," he affirmed. "Affection and tenderness can exist and work outside romance. Love can outlast passion. It need not die. It can survive, but only if it changes its character or, rather, it gains its real character." Romance, he believed, is preparation for "true love." When the emotional frenzy dies down, as "in the recovery process in cases of hysteria," idolatry can give way to appreciation of a real person and deepening affection. Then, Reik promised, "There may not be ecstasy or intoxication but there is an emotional companionship which cements the tie between two people, forming an intimacy which grows as they live together through the same joys and griefs."

Love or Limerence?

Dorothy Tennov, who analyzed romance from thrilling rise to dismal collapse, generally agreed with Reik that romance and love are different from each other. After gathering 1,100 questionnaires and then further information from 500 more people, she concluded that romance was so detached from real love that she coined another name for it: "limerence." The lilting term, capturing the charm of the experience, describes "first and foremost a condition of cognitive obsession," Tennov wrote. The lover is constantly preoccupied with the image of the beloved, who appears no ordinary person but unutterably wonderful, if not flawless.

With Reik, Tennov saw romance as no mere sexual attraction. Though sex is never absent from limerence, emotions demand much more. "The 'moment of consummation,' the goal, the climax of the limerence fantasy, is not sexual union," she observed, "but emotional commitment on the part of LO [limerent object]." In short, limerence wants heart and soul as well as body.

For limerence to exist, she found, two factors are necessary: (1) hope for reciprocation and (2) uncertainty of receiving it. If hope dies completely, so does limerence. If uncertainty ends in confident commitment, as in marriage, limerence fades away.

The statistical time frame of most limerent feelings is between eighteen and thirty-six months, reported Tennov (which recalls the love potion of Tristan and Isolde that, according to the legend, would unite a couple for three years). "My estimation of average limerent duration is approximately two years," Tennov calculated.

As limerence declines toward zero-point, ex-LOs either drift apart or replace their transient feelings with "the genuine love of affectional bonding." This companionate love is serene and rational, rather than desperate and frenzied. It also is marked by mutual concern and active care, rather than impassioned desire. "It is what is described as the hoped-for relationship between limerents after the honeymoon when the serious business of charting a common and compatible life course begins," Tennov concluded.

Romance and Pathology

Both Tennov and Reik held benign views of romance. They dealt with it gently even though they saw in it serious shortcomings. Other psychologists grant romance greater acceptance, seeing its present-day proliferation as a positive good or a practical need in a social climate of loneliness and insecurity. Some therapists, in fact, encountering people who never have fallen in love, diagnose their absence of romantic feeling as a sign of emotional problems. They interpret lack of falling in love as an inability to form normal love relationships and a serious pathological symptom needing long-term therapy.

A large number of social scientists take an opposite, strongly negative view of modern-style romance. Some brush it aside as a commercial product prepackaged and publicized by mass communications. Others see it as a distraction, a diversion, an aberration, an emotional booby trap devised by a sick society, a spin-off of mass pathology. A few psychiatrists treat lovesick patients with drugs that counteract natural amphetamines linked to infatuation in emotional centers of the brain—a kind of anti-love potion.

Psychologist M. Scott Peck claims that falling in love has nothing to do with real love:

> In some respects . . . the act of falling in love is an act of regression. The experience of merging with the loved one has its echoes from the time when we were merged with our mothers in infancy. Along with the merging, we also reexperience the sense of omnipotence we had to give up in our journey out of childhood. All things seem possible. United with our beloved, we feel we can conquer all obstacles. We believe that the strength of our love will cause the forces of opposition to bow down in submission and melt away into the darkness. All problems will be overcome. The future will be all light. The unreality of those feelings when we have fallen in love is essentially the same as the unreality of the two-year-old who feels itself to be king of the family and the world with power unlimited.

Some psychologists consider the state of "being in love" an obsession unconsciously motivated by forgotten angers, sibling rivalries, sadistic and masochistic tendencies, and similar emotional difficulties. Karen Horney regarded romantic love as a mark of a dependent personality deficient in self-esteem and basically masochistic, and romance itself as a pathological obsession. Other psychologists call our society's favorite kind of love "addiction," "morbid dependency," "perverted love," "erotomania," and "destructive passion."

The humanistic psychologist Maslow dismissed romance as so much blindness and dependency. He classified two contrasting types of love.

One he called D-love (deficiency), which amounts to need-love, selfish love. Normal for infants, D-love also is felt by emotionally immature adults as a hunger, an emptiness, a yearning to be filled. The D-lover's partner is valued instrumentally for his or her ability to satisfy hungers. D-love is dependent, anxious, jealous, and hostile when disappointed. Maslow's second type is B-love (being), a benevolent regard for the welfare of another person. This kind of love is less needful, less possessive, anxious only for the well-being of the beloved. People in B-love are independent and autonomous, free of jealousy, secure, generous, and eager to promote the well-being of the other person.

Dorothy Tennov points out that writers on romance often talk of madness (recalling the *theia mania* of the ancient Greeks and the "pleasing madness" of the thirteenth-century's Richard de Fournival). Tennov cited the nineteenth-century French psychological novelist Marie-Henri Beyle de Stendhal, who penned an astute analysis of romance and claimed that being swept away by love, no matter how painful, was life's most pleasurable experience; he also called it a disease.

Even Rousseau, though a founding father of modern romance, declared the form of love imaginary: "And what is true love itself if it is not chimera, lie, and illusion? We love the image we make for ourselves far more than we love the object to which we apply it."

The twentieth-century Spanish philosopher Jose Ortega y Gasset called falling in love "an inferior state of mind, a form of transitory imbecility." American actress Katherine Hepburn added, "Insanity may be grounds for divorce in some states but . . . it's grounds for marriage in all."

Psychoanalysts Karen Horney, Alfred Adler, and Sandor Ferenci, among others, regard the modern mode of romance as a serious menace to mental stability. Equally, say sociologists, it wreaks havoc with wedlock, since it launches couples suddenly into union then founders, leaving them stranded on an emotional desert island.

Anthropologist Robert Linton in 1936 wrote a caustic appraisal of modern romance that has become something of a classic in the field: "All societies recognize that there are occasional violent attachments between persons of opposite sex, but our present American culture is practically the only one which has attempted to capitalize these and make them the basis for marriage. . . . Their rarity in most societies suggests that they are psychological abnormalities to which our own culture has attached an extraordinary value just as other cultures have attached extreme values to other abnormalities. The hero of the modern American movie is always a romantic lover just as the hero of the old Arab epic is always an epileptic."

Harvard sociologist Pitirim Sorokin, who spent ten years of a remarkably productive career documenting the disintegration of modern Western culture, went on to found the Harvard Research Center in Creative Altruism to study the possibility of moral and mental regeneration in a confused and demoralized world. From his thinking and researches, he defined three levels of love:

✦ low-grade love of acquisitive desire
✦ natural love blending self-interest with benevolence
✦ unselfish altruistic love

The lowest love, he said, is an "egoistic experience" where "the other person is always only the *means* value." The third form was "genuine love," in which "the loved person is experienced always as the *end* value." He also deemed altruistic love "the highest life of humanity."

Sorokin, like Freud, also saw love in cosmic dimensions, declaring it a form of energy. Life itself is a form of love-energy, while love is the concentrated form of life. The basic polarity in all existing things is the universal force of love against strife and chaos. Love unifies, harmonizes, integrates, creates. It operates everywhere. Everything depends on love for existence. We see the physical counterpart of psychical love in the unity of the atom and the universe, Sorokin concluded.

Psychoanalyst Erich Fromm thought of love more as an art than a science. In his classic book *The Art of Loving,* he sees love as "the only sane and satisfactory solution" for the problem of human aloneness. In Fromm's interpretation, genuine love is not mere feeling but decision and promise, not only desire but "*active concern for the life and the growth of that which we love* [italics his]." Care, responsibility, respect, knowledge—these are among the traits of real love. "The art of loving requires discipline, concentration, patience, supreme concern, sensitivity," he wrote. "It should not be narcissistic, but objective, reasonable, humble, faithful, courageous, active, and dynamic."

With Sorokin, Fromm believed that the only love worth the name is the altruistic kind. And modern romance? Mere egotism *à deux*, or a symbiotic union of sadist devouring masochists! Fromm used alarming terms to decry the dearth of beneficent love in our time:

✦ "People capable of love, under the present system, are necessarily the exceptions," he wrote; "love is by necessity a marginal phenomenon in present-day Western society."

✦ "To analyze the nature of love is to discover its general absence today and to criticize the social conditions that are responsible for this absence."

✦ "There are many people . . . who have never seen a loving person. . . ."

✦ "No objective observer of our Western life can doubt that love— brotherly love, motherly love, and erotic love—is a relatively rare phenomenon, and that its place is taken by a number of forms of pseudo-love which are in reality so many forms of the disintegration of love."

Startling statements? Indeed they are! Yet a look at modern-style love reveals exactly that, while a close look at our lives shows the staggering damage the disintegration of love is causing.

Love Damaged

DO YOU . . . WISH TO KNOW THE CHARACTER OF A LOVE?
SEE WHERE IT LEADS.
—ST. AUGUSTINE OF HIPPO (354–430)

ARRANGEMENTS TO HOOK-UPS

ONCE UPON A TIME in France, Italy, Portugal, Russia, Spain, and other European countries, mating was an *affaire de famille* arranged by parents or professional brokers. Its purpose was not only to unite couples in wedlock but also to join families, lands, and fortunes.

Among Hasidic Jews, in much of the Islamic world, and in many Asian societies, marriages are still set up by elders. Where arranged marriage persists, young people readily accept the system. Visiting the West, they tend to pity rather than envy free romancers, seeing them as anxious, fretful, and pained. Meanwhile they trust that their parents will see them married promptly and well when the proper time arrives.

And what of love? Arranged matches do not mean to exclude love but only to precede it. The bride and groom, sometimes never meeting before their wedding, are expected to behave toward one another thereafter in a manner that generates love. As the seventeenth-century French playwright Jean Baptiste Molière observed, "Love is often a fruit of marriage." An Indonesian student of Hope College social psychologist David G. Myers, who would face arranged marriage when she returned home, expressed similar confidence: "I do believe if a person has a good heart, love will grow easily and beautifully."

Some years ago, when a traditional taboo against premarital sex still held firm in China, the wife of a Chinese minister to the United States was asked about her views on love and marriage. She had nothing good to say about Western romantic freedom. "Americans love, marry, and get divorced," she observed. "We marry, love, and get home and happiness and children. Which way you like?" Meanwhile people from India also attested, "First we marry, then we fall in love." In more recent years, however, Chinese and other Asian people striving to modernize have been taking on, along with other Western ways, our mode of loving. Where this occurs, adolescent dating, promiscuity, adultery, and prostitution rise, and they, too, love, marry, and divorce.

In Western culture, when young people turned away from arranged marriage in favor of liaisons of choice, they held a variety of goals. For some, friendship or high esteem was a sufficient reason to marry. Others sought romantic attraction. In any case, however, they pursued not passing fancies but serious courtship. A liaison that failed was a personal misfortune often leading to lifelong regret. Only in the twentieth century, when earnest "keeping company" gave way to serial dating, did love-seeking diminish to the trial relationship or emotional recreation that we accept as romance today.

Fairly soon after the beginning of dating, some social scientists branded it sham courtship. Willard Waller in 1937 coined the term "rating and dating complex," describing dating as a contest for racking up scores, girls by getting dates with high-status guys, boys by scoring sexually with as many girls as they could.

Anthropologist Margaret Mead went further, declaring dating not courtship at all but a loveless competition for personal feelings of popularity and success. She believed the system to be ultimately damaging to marriage.

In the 1950s, Samuel Lowrie, a sociologist at Bowling Green State College in Ohio, asked 1,595 high school and college males and females why they dated. In anonymous responses, one quarter cited competitive prestige, one third social education and self-improvement, and only a bit more than a third cited affection, courtship, and marriage. Since then the marriage element has vastly diminished in male-female connections.

Coupling when partners are too immature for tender relationships generally is flippant, ego-oriented, and loveless. Fledgling daters come together awkwardly, experimentally, to eat ice cream, dance, go to movies, "suck face," "cop feels," and generally see what can be had. Later, couples become more emotionally questing. Ultimately, matching turns practical and cautious as people try to form more enduring relationships.

Yet lasting love has become a quest so unsure that long-range hopes might seem an invitation to despair. In response to that uncertainty, relationships since the 1980s have turned more tentative still. Dating, itself a mere skeleton of courtship, has given way to a bevy of vague and confusing couplings: from boyfriend-girlfriend, to living together, to random "hooking up" for a night of deliberately uncommitted sex.

In an age of AIDS and rampant sexual diseases of other kinds, romancers feel all the more reason for hesitation. Relationships can take on the intrigue of a cloak-and-dagger drama. "So tell me," asks a wary partner, "how long did you go with your last boy/girl friend? Mmm, I see. And did you have many before that?"

ROMANTIC DEVASTATION

Our society customarily has portrayed romance as charming, enchanting, and sweet. Sober researchers long have said otherwise. As early as 1945, two University of Minnesota sociologists investigated some 900 campus love affairs and discovered that about half of them resulted in serious emotional trauma. Decades later, psychologist and author Dorothy Tennov reported that more than half the subjects of her wide surveys of romance suffered emotional depression, while more than twenty-five percent admitted to suicidal thoughts. Some had seriously tried to kill themselves.

How much anguish from hidden heartbreak surrounds us we can only wonder. "Loss of a loved person," psychiatrist John Bowlby notes, "is one of the most intensely painful experiences any human being can suffer."

I personally have known several young women who attempted suicide after broken-off love-sex affairs. One cut her wrists. Another swallowed a bottle of aspirin. The third, between her nineteenth and twenty-first years, smashed a car into an earthmover, survived in spite of injuries, then overdosed on barbiturates, surviving again when her roommate came home and found her unconscious on the floor.

I've asked young women about failed relationships, "Did you tell him [the ex-boyfriend] how you were hurting?"

Definitely not! came the answer.

"Did you tell your parents?"

No again. Some told a sister or special girlfriend. But many people injured by romance live alone with their confusion and anguish—and sometimes pregnancy, abortion, or suicide attempts.

"Our society overlooks the drain on emotional balance that results from severing attachments," observes *A General Theory of Love*, a book authored by psychiatrists Thomas Lewis, Fari Amini, and Richard Lannon. Adds psychologist Tennov, "My research suggests strongly that the negative aspects of limerence [romantic love] have not been given the kind of recognition that they deserve." They are, in fact, one of the most burdensome, agonized, and best-kept secrets in our society.

ROMANCE VS. MARRIAGE

People generally have assumed that a prime purpose of romance is preparation for marriage. Yet the linkage is loose at best. Sociologists Elaine H. and G. William Walster of the University of Wisconsin found that ninety-seven percent of American men and women fell in love one or more times by their late teens—and most of them fell out again within two years. Other studies show that the typical American has from seven to ten romances over the course of a lifetime.

A study of courtship patterns among 400 college students found that, of 582 love affairs, nearly three-fourths ended without marriage. Another researcher found that only fifteen percent of the relationships he recorded led to wedlock.

While courtships of prior generations were focused on the future and were meant to end in nuptials, current liaisons are universally acknowledged to be provisional and temporary. It should be no surprise, then, that much of modern marriage also turns out to be provisional and temporary, a simple case of practice shaping performance.

Modern romance, with its casual bonds, ready sexual liaisons, and frequent break-ups, turns out to be more a form of emotional and physical promiscuity than preparation for commitment. As such, it seeds the deterioration of marriage, equipping people better for the progressive polygamy of unmarried cohabitation, adultery, divorce, remarriage, and further divorce than for lifelong devotion and fidelity in enduring matrimony. As Denis de Rougemont, a Swiss philosophical thinker on the subject of love, puts it: ". . . love, *as understood nowadays* [italics his], is the flat negation of the marriage to which it is claimed that this love can serve as support."

Many aspects of our model of romance have an eroding effect upon marriage. Presenting a false self is one of its most hazardous customs. Psychologist Sidney M. Jourard observes: "People marry for many reasons, and few people marry for love, because few people are able to love the person they marry at the time they marry them. In our society, people commonly marry in a romantic haze, usually ignorant of the traits, needs, and aims of their spouses. They marry an image, not a person. The image is partly a construction of their own needs and fantasies . . . and partly a result of deliberate ambiguity or contrivance on the part of the other. The other person presents himself as the kind of person he thinks will be loved and accepted, but it is seldom really him. Following the ceremony, reality often sets in with an unpleasant shock."

Inevitably a heart full of illusion leads to disillusion—a byword in modern romance and marriage. Additionally, the many emotional games, strategies, and tactics of romance can turn wedlock into a contest of self-seeking, if not outright combat.

Meanwhile, the hurts of past romances carry over, straining each new relationship from the start. A police lineup of past partners primes troubles of many kinds, from lying and jealousy to suspicion and distrust.

Romancing couples seriously possess each other in the sense of holding claims to one another's hearts. Sexual contact bonds them all the tighter. Though affairs might pass away, they do not fade into the past to be forgotten like a blissful summer day or a miserable case of the flu. Instead, as psychologist Martin Bloom testifies, "a love experience leaves a strong impression which never entirely dies out." Often belatedly, lovers discover that sex is a lifetime bonding experience, as unremovable as a trauma. A middle-aged, unmarried woman once told me, "Our former loves are engraved on our souls."

Many married couples will sadly attest that premarital sex affairs weaken the emotional bonding power of physical union in wedlock. Serial sex-romancers forfeit the uniqueness of the one act that can distinguish marriage from all other forms of association.

Sigmund Freud, the father of psychoanalysis, stressed the link between sex and bonding, especially in regard to women. In a little-known paper titled "The Taboo of Virginity," the Austrian doctor observed that when a woman gives all of her chastity to one man, she takes him "into a close and lasting relationship which will never again be available to any other man." She establishes a deep emotional bond that delivers her into powerful and involuntary devotion. This attachment is strong enough to lead her, in Freud's terms, to "the heaviest sacrifices of personal interests."

Psychologically she might never be able to free herself from the profound effects of the encounter. This helps her to withstand "new impressions and temptations" from other men. It also stands in the way of future intimate relationships. If she tries to turn her love to another man, the image of the first—even if she no longer loves him—rises as a barrier. Freud added that this surge of devotion accompanying a first giving of chastity "is indeed indispensable in maintaining civilized marriage and restraining the polygamous tendencies that threaten to undermine it. . . ."

Later psychologists also have remarked on the deep attachment women can feel toward their first sex partner. The feminist Simone de Beauvoir acknowledged in a more general way in her book *The Second Sex* that "psychiatrists all agree on the extreme importance of a woman's first erotic experiences: their repercussions are felt throughout the rest of her life."

Writer and sociologist Barbara Defoe Whitehead observes in her book *Why Are There No Good Men Left?*, "Some women still refer to their first boyfriend as 'my one true love,' and they seem almost shy when they say it." Researchers from the University of London reported in 2003 that women who married the first man they had a relationship with enjoyed the best mental health among people of their gender, while women who experienced several relationships and splits suffered the worst emotional well-being.

In other times and places sexual liberality has been demonstrably damaging to lasting love, marriage, and emotional satisfaction. As Freud noted elsewhere, "It can be easily shown that the psychical value of erotic needs is reduced as their satisfaction becomes easy. . . . This is true of both individuals and of nations. In times in which there were no difficulties standing in the way of sexual satisfaction, such as perhaps during the decline of the ancient civilizations, love became worthless and life empty."

A survey of the present-day world also suggests a link between premarital chastity and marital solidity. As a global traveler for many decades, I observed from culture to culture that the looser the sex the looser marriage tends to be. I found an ultimate example of this in the mid-Pacific islands of French Polynesia. On one remote island, a Protestant circuit minister newly arrived from the West was horrified to find many people living in sin and insisted that all cohabiting adults be married. The islanders, an easygoing people, genially consented. When the minister returned a year later, he was shocked to find that most of his newlyweds were living with somebody else. On another island, a conscientious Catholic priest refused to marry couples until they had a brace of children to prove the union would last. He reasoned that living in sin was less sinful than adultery.

According to Harvard sociologist Pitirim Sorokin, all civilized cultures at their times of flourishing and strong social institutions restricted sexual practices. Also investigating cultural stability, the scholar J. D. Unwin in his book *Sex and Culture* found parallels between monogamy and the health of civilization in eighty-six societies— including Sumerian, Babylonian, Greek, Roman, Moorish, and modern Western culture. Without exception, he reported, these societies flourished in times of sexual fidelity, declined when sexual mores loosened, and rose again if firm standards were revived.

In all fairness, though, it seems wise to take an anthropologist's point of view and recognize sex as but one among many interlinked moral factors that guides a culture upward or leads it into decline. It seems sufficient to conclude that romance as we do it damages people emotionally and works against stable marriage.

Love Lost

TRÍ NÍDO CHÍM TRÍD AN NGRÁ,/
AN PEACA, AN BÁS IS AN PHIAN.
(THREE THINGS I SEE THROUGH LOVE,/
THE ACT OF SIN, DEATH AND PAIN.)
—IRISH POEM

IN THE SELF-PREOCCUPATION that romance generates, we often focus less on the effects it is having on the broader society around us. Yet the consequences of our ineffective style of loving ripple outward far beyond ourselves, changing other people's lives and collectively reshaping our whole culture.

The human losses, as tabulated in academic studies, dramatized in the media, and recounted in our neighborhoods and families, are colossal. If damage to lives and disruption to the society somehow could be tallied up, our common problems with love would be ranked among the major disasters of our time. Beyond personal misfortunes, failures in love are directly responsible for waning wedlock, the disintegration of the family, child deprivations, and ever growing, ever broadening social dysfunction.

MARRIAGE IN DECAY

After damaged souls, the prime casualty of modern-style love is marriage.

"Marriage is a cultural universal," writes anthropologist Helen E. Fisher. "It predominates in every society in the world." Not only can marriage offer companionship and ease the loads of life, it also is irreplaceable for raising children and perpetuating future generations.

The 1948 United Nations Universal Declaration of Human Rights states that "the family is the natural and fundamental group unit of society." Added anthropologist Margaret Mead, "No matter how many communes anybody invents, the family always creeps back."

Presently, however, the blood-tie family unit is slipping away as one more victim of ineffectual love. As a study from the University of Chicago points out: "Marriage has declined as the central institution under which households are organized and children are raised."

"Americans are marrying less and a growing number will never marry," says a report from the Duquesne University Family Institute. In 1960, nearly sixty-eight percent of all people of marriageable age were wed. Midway into the first decade of the twenty-first century, only fifty percent were married.

In most times and cultures, marriage is more a social relationship than a private and personal arrangement. It assures the community that partners intend to stay together and nurture their offspring. This view of marriage sees it designed less for the individual pleasure and convenience of adults than for the security of the whole society and the assurance of its future. To this end, the *Book of Common Prayer* of 1549 led wedded partners, "To have and to hold from this day forward, for better for worse, for richer for poorer, in sickness and in health, to love and to cherish, till death do us part."

Amen? Not anymore. Once upon a time, marriage was regarded as the supreme sacrifice of self. Now that's reversed and wedlock is sought as a supreme fulfillment of self. With generous love lacking and the desire to acquire taking its place, commitments are bound to wear thin.

Some current wedding ceremonies freely acknowledge the fragility of modern dedication, asking only for a transient bond: "as long as we both shall love." The assumption is that love gets misplaced like an earring, slips off the hook like a wriggly fish, functions independently beyond anyone's control, a matter of chance instead of choice. "Till change of heart do us part" unlocks wedlock to become just another sex-love affair as erratic as a shipboard romance, a day-at-a-time proposition, a notarized date, a liaison of convenience that plans in advance for a life of alternating passion and lovelessness.

Our society, equally loveless in principle, strives to accommodate this feeble mode of wedlock. In the mid-1990s, the Council on Families in America issued a startling report titled "Marriage in America." The council included eighteen scholars and social historians, among them Jean Bethke Elshtain, professor of social and political ethics at the University of Chicago; sociologist David Popenoe of Rutgers University; and etiquette expert Judith "Miss Manners" Martin. Jointly they asserted: "Marriage is under assault in our society. It is an institution in decline and even disrepute." While the social order ridicules the happy family as a holdover from 1950s television shows, marriage is depicted as restrictive, confining, oppressive. At the same time, wedlock is demoted from a vital social institution to merely one more lifestyle preference among many.

Meanwhile, marriages "are becoming more difficult, fragile, and unhappy," according to the council. A vast and growing body of evidence indicates that the quality of married life in the United States took a sharp downward turn long ago. Though recent trends suggest that the plunge might be leveling off, the prominent demographer Kingsley Davis nonetheless attests, "at no time in history, with the possible exception of Imperial Rome, has the institution of marriage been more problematic than it is today."

Nor is the problem confined to America. Virtually everywhere in the Western world family separation is on the rise. "The very basis of the family has changed," concludes a demographic report on fifteen European Union countries. "The family, in the past an institution and means of integration, has become a pact between two individuals looking for personal fulfillment." François Begeot, a social scientist at the European Union's statistical office in Luxembourg, reported, "People want happiness now. It's an individual thing. They now are far less willing to sacrifice for larger obligations or duties."

With partners unwilling to invest time, resources, hopes, and commitment in lifelong marriage, the arrangement stands or falls on whether it produces sufficient happiness. This is a fragile basis for the existence of anything. When "till death do us part" is replaced by "as long as I am happy," the quest for personal fulfillment and individual autonomy transforms a onetime culture of marriage and family into a society of infidelity, divorce, and displaced children.

PRIMED FOR ADULTERY

While modern romancing masquerades as preparation for marriage, it functions better as training for infidelity. Regrettably for researchers, as a 2003 report from the National Opinion Research Center at the University of Chicago states, "There are probably more scientifically worthless 'facts' on extramarital relations than on any other facet of human behavior." Yet there has been no shortage of attempts to tally the unfaithful.

During the sexual revolution of the 1920s, psychiatrist Gilbert Hamilton, a trailblazing sex researcher, disclosed that 28 of 100 men he interviewed and 24 of 100 women had committed adultery. In the late 1940s and early 1950s, the biologist Alfred Kinsey and his associates reported that more than one-third of all husbands among 6,427 men interviewed had violated their wedding vows. He went on to deem those figures low, believing that many subjects had concealed their dereliction. The real figure, he estimated, stood closer to half. And women? Kinsey reported that 26 percent of 6,972 had been unfaithful to their husbands by age forty.

Later social scientists have cast doubt on Kinsey's research methods. Still more they might question any broad application of a 1970s *Playboy* magazine survey that found 41 percent of 691 men and 25 percent of 740 married, white, middle-class women straying from marital fidelity, and straying earlier in marriage than before. Similarly, a 1980s survey of 106,000 readers of *Cosmopolitan* magazine claiming 54 percent of married women had engaged in at least one extramarital affair might be taken to reflect the sex-oriented periodical's readership. A *Cosmopolitan* poll of 7,239 men that reported adultery among 72 percent of those married more than two years seems to have equally limited application.

Marriage and Divorce Today claimed in 1987, "Seventy percent of all

Americans engage in an affair sometime during their marital life." In 1993, *The Janus Report on Sexual Behavior* pegged the number considerably lower: thirty-five percent of men, twenty-six percent of women. A 1996 *Newsweek* magazine poll reported thirty-six percent of its respondents saying some or most of the married people they knew had pursued extramarital affairs, while young wives were less faithful than young husbands.

Perhaps more reliable is a report from the National Opinion Research Center citing that about fifteen to eighteen percent of married people have had a sexual partner other than their spouse while married. "The rates of extramarital relations are about twice as high among husbands as among wives," the report added. Interestingly, according to the eminent sociologist Norval Glenn, since the 1970s, "disapproval of extramarital sex relations has increased substantially in this country."

In any case, whichever survey we believe or doubt, it seems likely that philandering is a common pastime in our social milieu.

In a study of 160 societies, anthropologist Laura Betzig found that overt philandering is the commonest reason for divorce. Many of the world's societies of past and present have punished adulterers by social ostracism, public whipping, branding, beating, genital mutilation, amputation of nose and ears, and death by choking, drowning, stabbing, and stoning. Though our society goes relatively easy on disloyal marriage partners, adultery remains a major cause for both family violence and divorce in America and throughout the Western world.

A Culture of Divorce

During much of humankind's agrarian past, divorce was uncommon. It was rare in ancient Israel. Greeks of the Homeric age permitted divorce but did it seldom. Later classical Greeks experimented with various forms of extramarital sex but banned practices that might jeopardize family stability. For example, a man could not bring his mistress home.

In Rome's earlier, republican days, marital dissolution was infrequent. Only in later times, as cities grew and women could gain wealth and independence, did divorce split couples among the upper classes.

For rural Christians, divorce remained rare both before and after the fall of Rome. In medieval Europe, divorce was unusual. It remained so until the Industrial Revolution.

In England of early industrial days, divorce law was so restrictive and the method so expensive that only 184 divorces were granted between 1715 and 1852. In Catholic France, divorce was abolished by the Napoleonic Code of laws.

The divorce rate began to rise in many Western countries around the middle of the nineteenth century. Since then it has grown by lurches and leaps. Between 1925 and 1975, for example, divorces in the United States soared more than sevenfold. In the decade from 1966 to 1976 alone the rate doubled. Divorce reached a high point in 1981. Now it stands at historically record levels approaching fifty percent. According to retired Princeton University family historian Lawrence Stone, "The scale of marital breakdowns in the West since 1960 has no historical precedent that I know of, and seems unique. There has been nothing like it for the past 2,000 years, and probably longer."

As late as 1962, almost half the respondents in one American survey said parents should stay together for the sake of their offspring even if they did not get along. By 1985, only eighteen percent believed this. Now people part because love ebbs away, or because they feel unhappy, or because they have found someone else, with far less regard for any children involved.

Though people joke about "the seven-year itch," United Nations demographic yearbooks, published since 1947, show divorce reaching a general peak around the fourth year after marriage. This applies more or less equally in sixty-two countries as culturally disparate as Venezuela, Finland, South Africa, Russia, and Egypt. As marriages age, divorces gradually decline. This remains true whether the divorce rate in the culture is low or high, suggesting a cross-cultural pattern of marital decay and endurance.

In the United States, the prime time for divorce tends to hover below four years after the wedding, and at times as low as two or three years. This recalls again the love potion of Tristan and Isolde that held enough potency to unite a couple for three years. It also corresponds with psychologist Dorothy Tennov's statistics citing the normal duration of romantic love between eighteen and thirty-six months.

Divorce peaks among the young. At least three-quarters of all divorces separate people under forty-five. With advancing age, in the United States as elsewhere, divorce diminishes.

Couples most likely to part have different values, habits, interests, and leisure activities. Divorce rates rise higher in cities, among non-churchgoers, and when a wife's income is larger than the husband's. Estrangements lessen with the number of offspring, though a growing proportion involves couples with young children.

Normally divorcees need two to four years to work through the travails of emotional disconnection, the average time being closer to the full four years. The vast majority marry again, about half within three years. In the United States among divorced people, eighty percent of men and seventy-five percent of women take other spouses. Second marriages have a higher rate of divorce than first marriages.

Though people of the United States have been setting global records for divorce, a report from the Population Council, a New York-based demographic institute, finds marriages around the world dissolving with increasing frequency. The overall divorce rate in industrialized countries doubled between 1970 and 1990, with Sweden, Denmark, Great Britain, and Canada rivaling the United States. In the world's developing countries, among women who have reached the age of forty, roughly one fourth of all marriages have dissolved.

Meanwhile the society, abandoning hope of reducing divorce, looks for ways to live with it more comfortably. Some lawyers advise preparedness for divorce as part of preparation for marriage, with terms of a possible future split worked out in a prenuptial agreement. Marriage therapists counselling troubled couples often shift their focus toward the goal of "a good divorce." One pastor in Bradford, England, offered a divorce ceremony as "a service of healing." Meanwhile, a whole industry has grown up around broken marriage, with therapists, lawyers, tax experts, and greeting card companies reaping the bounty. With the

Internet came do-it-yourself, mouse-click divorce costing $50 to $1,000 for paperwork and services through such Web sites as LegalZoom and DivorceWizzards.

We are admonished that the term "broken home" is politically incorrect, cruel to everyone involved. We are assured that any group of people—from mother and child to a love commune—can be a family by definition, and one is as good as another. We are urged to provide children with positive and empowering images of the situations that divorce plunges them into—which can range from love without fixed structure to neglect or exploitation. Meanwhile, the society instructs us to improve post-divorce relations with better communication, cooperation, and amiability—the precise lack of which leads to divorce to begin with.

Governments, believing that nothing can stem the tide of estrangement, resort to damage control. They replace fatherhood with child maintenance payments, support for marriage with divorce reform, and parenthood with foster care and group homes. Some people fear that traditional wedlock is likely to be rare within another generation or so. Historians say that such extremely high levels of divorce are not only historically unusual but also commonly associated with overall social breakdown.

"The divorce revolution," says the Council on Families in America, "set out to achieve some worthy goals: to foster greater equality between men and women, to improve the family lives of women, and to expand individual happiness and choice." But the revolution proved largely destructive, with devastating results for both adults and children: a lessening of individual happiness, economic insecurity for women, isolation for men, and for children sadness, rage, and about double the odds that they, too, will end up divorced.

DOWN WITH MARRIAGE

Where men and women of the past were eager to marry, young people of the present feel wary. Many coming out of divorced families are painfully conscious of the fragility of modern wedlock. Though youth often still admit a keen desire to wed, the married state seems rife with menace and built-in prospects for failure.

Some young people hedge their bets, marriage counsellors say, by searching for virtual clones of themselves, with tastes, preferences, hopes, and dreams as identical to their own as possible. Others seek not so much a working marriage as an alliance promising comfort and security in an alien and hostile world. Some people give up on marriage altogether to stay out of harm's way.

Says the Council on Families, "Relationships between men and women are not getting better; by many measures, they are getting worse." The mere meeting of the sexes, once upheld by character and trust, now is undermined by suspicion, competition, and violence. A report cited in *Harper's Magazine* indicated that forty-nine percent of women believe their car is more reliable than a man. And when men ask the question, "Would I want her to be the mother of my children?" they answer in the negative with dismaying frequency.

Family life has lost much of its appeal. No longer is the home a man's castle, a woman's refuge, and the loving and secure cradle of the race. Motherhood, once the most honored of all professions, has fallen drastically out of vogue in general society. Conceivably, the media's glamorizing of celebrity pregnancies might suggest a reversal of this trend, restoring motherhood as a stylish option for today's woman. Meanwhile, however, one survey found only seven percent of United States women agreeing that a home and children are what women really want in life.

Many mothers who stay at home to take care of their offspring feel somehow in disgrace: non-workers, non-contributors, underdeveloped individuals, possessors of little status or personal identity, vaguely subversive. "I feel pressure to go back to work," admitted a mother quoted in a *Reader's Digest* article by feminist Betty Friedan. "I dread that inevitable question at parties, 'What do you do?'"

Children, in the meantime, sometimes are less bundles of joy than expendable frills: one more item in a life of acquisition, a domestic hobby to round out personal existence, a means of having company. "I was the first woman in management here," said an older woman quoted by Friedan in her *Reader's Digest* article. "I gave everything to the job.

It was exciting at first. Now there's devastating loneliness. Maybe I should have a kid, even without a husband. I can't stand going home alone every night."

Economists regularly portray children as a staggering burden. A still less kindly view portrays the nation's tykes, in any but carefully limited numbers, as an excessive strain upon the ecosphere, a kind of fleshly pollution. A solid majority of American households now have no children at home, a fact only partly attributable to later marriages and empty nests. By 2002, according to the National Center for Health Statistics, America's birth rate had fallen to a record low.

Meanwhile, the United States marriage rate for single women between the ages of fifteen and forty-four has plummeted to an all-time low, and women in their prime childbearing years are choosing to have fewer children. In England and Wales, marriage rates have halved over the past century, while brides and grooms are getting older. In Western Europe, the number of marriages has decreased by forty percent during the past generation. Rates of marriages and births have plunged also in several Eastern European countries. Demographers expect the marriage rate to drop still further in the foreseeable future.

In what some people are calling the "postmarital society," single-person residences form the fastest-growing category of households in the Western world. In the 1950s, only ten percent of all homes in the United States consisted of one person. By the mid-1990s, the figure had climbed to more than twenty-five percent. In Sweden, the comparable figure soars at nearly forty percent.

Up with Cohabitation

In a *Redbook* magazine article of July 1966, anthropologist Margaret Mead proposed a startling solution for rising divorce rates: a two-step system of marriage. Step one she called "individual marriage," a legal tie that implied no lifelong commitment, excluded children, and imposed no economic consequences if the match broke up. Step two, "parental marriage," was to be a legal and long-term bond with provisions made for children in event of divorce.

Western society has settled on a form of her step one to meet the frequent failure of enduring love. Since 1970, the once scandalous act of "living together" has become routine in the United States, with the number of cohabiting couples rising 1,000 percent by 2005, from fewer than 500,000 to more than 4.7 million. Women born after 1963 are ten times more likely than women born thirty years earlier to live with a partner before marriage. By 1999, more than half of all first marriages were preceded by cohabitation. The most common living arrangement now is a household of unmarried people with no children. Meanwhile, reports from the National Marriage Project of Rutgers University observe that cohabitation before marriage coincides with weak wedlock. According to the Duquesne University Family Institute, people who live together before marrying are twice as likely to break up afterward.

For people wanting family atmosphere without commitment, multi-adult households have increased in recent years. In some associations unrelated friends become what sociologists call "fictive kin," even to the point of assigning roles to one another, as "mom," "dad," "brother," "sister," "aunt." Such fictive families are fulfilling social and economic needs for the first time in recorded history, springing up among young and old, able and disabled, prosperous and homeless. One New Jersey judge ruled that six college students on summer vacation constituted a family.

Solitary Parentage

Not long ago, a young man who made his girlfriend pregnant felt obliged to marry her and help raise their child. No longer. Now feral fathers roam the land in great number, having fun but not hanging around to pick up the tab. Some teenage studs brag about the number of girls they impregnate and the babies they randomly sire.

In 1960, nonmarital births in the United States stood at a modest 5.3 percent. Before the end of the century in both America and northern Europe, about one-third of all babies were born out of wedlock. In Sweden, Norway, and Denmark, the corresponding figure hovered around one-half.

Unwed parenthood has reached virtual parity with divorce as a generator of fatherless homes in the United States. From 1960 to 1995, the illegitimate birth rate in the country rose by more than fourfold. Especially significant about this trend is that many single women having children remain single. Some people, in fact, have come to celebrate single motherhood as a statement of liberation and independence, even though the vast majority of single mothers live under harsh economic pressure and emotional strain and say they would prefer a two-parent home.

The number of households maintained by women with no males present increased threefold between 1950 and the mid-1990s. In the United States, almost half of all children do not reside with both biological parents. A 1999 University of Chicago report forecast that in the twenty-first century children living with both original parents will be a minority.

In the growing culture of non-marriage, fathers often have been deemed unnecessary, irrelevant, and superfluous, except as a source of income. Yet social research strongly suggests that life without father can be perilous for children and the community at large.

More than half a century ago, the pioneering anthropologist Bronislaw Malinowski wrote: "In all human societies the father is regarded by tradition as indispensable . . . no child should be brought into the world without a man—and one man at that—assuming the role of sociological father, that is, guardian and protector, the male link between the child and the rest of the community." A 2001 report from the University of Connecticut covering fifty-two years of studies goes farther, saying, "In some analyses, the need for mother's love drops off, while the love of fathers takes precedent."

Data collected for the United States Department of Health and Human Services on thousands of children supports the need for two parents. Children with only one parent, whether through divorce or illegitimacy, are two to three times as prone to emotional or behavioral problems, and half again as likely to endure learning disabilities, as those who live with both parents. The data also indicate that teenage girls who grow up without fathers tend to start sexual activity earlier. A fifteen-year-old who lives with only her mother is three times as apt to lose her virginity before her sixteenth birthday as one who lives with two parents.

Rutgers sociologist David Popenoe cites "a strong likelihood that the increase in the number of fatherless children . . . has been a prominent factor in the growth of violence and juvenile delinquency." A survey done for the United States Justice Department of 14,000 prison inmates showed that more than half grew up in homes lacking two parents. Of all juveniles confined for violent crimes, more than seventy percent grew up without two parents. United States government social scientists William Galston and Elaine Kamarck add that the connection between crime and a father absent from the home "is so strong that [it] erases the relationship between race and crime and between low income and crime."

A mountain of evidence proclaims that children from single-parent families are more vulnerable to all kinds of harm, at all income levels, in all racial groups, under all conditions than children with both parents. Charles Murray, author of a celebrated critique of the welfare system titled *Losing Ground*, claims that illegitimacy "is the single most important social problem of our time—more important than crime, drugs, poverty, illiteracy, or homelessness because it drives everything else." When fatherless boys grow numerous in a community, he says, "the values of unsocialized male adolescents—physical violence, immediate gratification, and predatory sex—are made norms."

Psychologists additionally point out that without a father to provide a model of abstract authority, a child is less likely to develop the self-control of personal morality and will need external constraints to keep him under reasonable control and feeling secure. This becomes a natural invitation to peer pressure today and a police state or dictatorship tomorrow.

Suffer, The Children

In the love-lacking atmosphere of modern society, children find less of a warm welcome than they need to grow well and thrive.

Increasingly both men and women are struggling to avoid the

responsibilities naturally linked with sexual acts. As one commentator put it, "Single adults in America display a remarkable tendency to multiply without being fruitful." The 1973 Supreme Court case of Roe vs. Wade ratified the notion that bodily acts in themselves do not constitute personal or moral commitment. A woman becomes a mother only if she explicitly consents to be.

Males who would prefer the obligations of fatherhood to end with conception also can take comfort in the principle of Roe vs. Wade, feeling, not altogether unreasonably, that their bodily acts should not constitute commitment either. With the single-parent family now readily accepted, the no-parent family seems foreseeable, with offspring turned over to state institutions. Current commercial nurseries and day-care centers are a strong step in that direction.

Meanwhile, today's children experience a dizzying range of parentage. We see the stay-at-home Mom; the self-fulfilling career Mom; the necessarily working Mom; the overloaded divorced or never-married Mom. Fathers include the traditional patriarchal Dad who stands in social disfavor; the absentee Dad; the tenderized, sensitized, mother's-helper Dad who functions like another woman in the house; the Dad who pays child support and does not make trouble; the weekend good-time Dad; the deadbeat Dad who does not want to pay; the vanished biological father; the stepfather who might be kind and dutiful or negligent, cruel, and abusive; the live-in guy or chain of live-in guys.

Filling in during the absence of parents is a broad range of babysitters, day-care workers, foster parents, and other surrogates who some specialists on child welfare decry as a dismal substitute for loving fathers and mothers. As the Council on Families reasons:

> The parental relationship is unique in human affairs. In most social relationships, the reciprocity of benefits is carefully monitored, since any imbalance is regarded as exploitative. But in the parental relationship, as has often been pointed out, "the flow of benefits is prolongedly, cumulatively, and ungrudgingly unbalanced." Who is willing to make this kind of massive, unbalanced investment in children? Evolutionary biologists tell us that, without question, pair-bonded biolog-

ical parents are by far the most willing and the most highly motivated to the task. . . . No amount of public investment in children can possibly offset the private disinvestment that has accompanied the decline of marriage.

Because marriage is in serious trouble, so are children. Opinion polls in the United States indicate that most Americans believe family stress lies at the heart of the distress of the country's younger generation. Ample empirical evidence indicates that when marriages fail and families founder, children tend to grow up—or grow downward—generally disadvantaged.

The British Medical Journal in May 1998 noted that parenting is probably the most important public health issue facing our society. It was the single largest variable implicated in childhood diseases and accidents, teenage pregnancy and drug abuse, truancy, school disruption and underachievement, child abuse, unemployability, juvenile crime, and mental illness.

Deterioration in the welfare of children is equally reflected by United States statistics on everything from poverty, early school-leaving, teen pregnancies, gangs, and drug abuse to depression, suicide, and homicide. Violent crime among juveniles increased sixfold between 1960 and 1992, though it tapered off substantially in the decade after 1993.

In 2003, the National Campaign to Prevent Teen Pregnancy reported that twenty percent of adolescents experience sexual intercourse before age fifteen, and one in seven of the fourteen-year-old girls involved has been pregnant. With contraceptive use, abstinence programs, and worries about AIDS and other sexual diseases, teen pregnancy has been falling since 1993. Yet the United States still leads the world in teen pregnancy and birthrate, which in the early years of the new millennium represented 11.5 percent of all births in the nation.

A 1999 report from the United States Department of Health and Human Services says an estimated twenty-one percent of the nation's children aged nine to seventeen suffer a diagnosable mental or addictive disorder. The United States Centers for Disease Control conducting a study of 16,000 high school students found an astonishing one in twelve claimed to have attempted suicide in the previous year. Suicide presently is the third leading cause of death for fifteen- to twenty-four-year-olds. Alcoholism and eating disorders among the young have sky-rocketed.

The statistical prevalence of poverty has shifted from the elderly to the young. Some eighty percent of child poverty occurs among youth with broken families or unwed parents. Children raised by never-married mothers are seven times more likely to live in poverty than those raised by married, biological parents.

Children of fragmented families also are more apt to suffer vocational, emotional, and relational instability as adults. A major study reported in Britain's *The Lancet* medical journal in 2003 tracked some one million children for a decade into their mid-twenties and found those growing up in single-parent families twice as likely to develop serious psychiatric illness and addictions later in life.

In a reasonably healthy society, adults are vitally concerned with protecting and nurturing the young. In our sick-hearted society, we are constantly on guard against people who would devour the young.

In the 1980s, the once unmentionable sins of child abuse and incest became openly recognized as serious social problems in the United States. Reports of child neglect and abuse quintupled between 1976, when data were first collected, and 1995, when they reached some three million cases per year. Better reporting was one reason. More abuse is most likely another.

Between 1985 and 1992, fatalities from child abuse rose fifty-four percent nationwide. About two-thirds of the injuries involve the head, neck, and mouth. Parents or other caretakers killed mostly babies, toddlers, and preschoolers by shaking, beating, suffocating, stamping, drowning, scalding, severe dehydration, gradual starvation, or abandonment to medical neglect.

A *Los Angeles Times* poll taken as early as 1985 determined that twenty-two percent of all Americans had been victims of child sexual molestation. Recent survey data show that as many as sixty-two percent of pregnant teenagers suffered sexual abuse, most often by adult men, including fathers, stepfathers, stepbrothers, mothers' boyfriends, or other male family acquaintances.

Nor is the problem of sexual molestation unique to the United States. The most extensive study of child sexual abuse in Canada, as reported by Ottawa's National Clearinghouse on Family Violence, indicates that, among adult Canadians, fifty-three percent of women and thirty-one percent of men were sexually abused when they were children. *The Medical Journal of Australia* reports that thirty-five percent of women surveyed revealed some sexual abuse or experience that was unwanted or distressing during childhood. According to Britain's National Society for the Prevention of Cruelty to Children, the incidence of child sexual abuse in Britain stands at twenty-one percent for females, eleven percent for males; in Ireland, thirty percent for females and twenty-four percent for males; in Switzerland, thirty-nine percent for females and eleven percent for males. Though accurate figures for child sexual abuse are notoriously hard to come by, the incidence of the offense appears to be soaring everywhere figures are gathered. David Pithers of Britain's National Children's Home says that "sexual abuse has reached epidemic proportions" and is more common than physical abuse.

Some social scientists, analyzing the general atrophy of the loving family, fear for the future of the society at large. As early as 1975, psychologist Urie Bronfenbrenner of Cornell University pooled routine government statistics on birth, education, labor, marriage, household composition, divorce, and morality and concluded, "the system for making human beings in this society is breaking down." Psychiatrist Murray Bowen of Georgetown University predicted also in 1975 that the year would "look like the 'good old days' compared with times that are coming for society and the family." Social analysts anticipate that many of today's neglected children will grow into tomorrow's thugs, bringing on a descending night of ever increasing crime and violence.

WE ALL NEED LOVE

We all—ourselves, our children, our nation, our society—need love. It seems reasonable to say that without effective love our culture stands in danger of disintegrating.

Does this mean we need love in greater quantity? In a sense, yes. But we do not need more of what we have now: no more pathological romance, no more Cupid's arrow as a thorn in the flesh, no more poisoned apples of self-seeking love, no more high-risk activities of the heart, no more love as systematic torment.

We do not need more consumer-romance preparing people for marital failure, sowing chaos and emotional famine in its wake. The sick society continues to promote this mode of love, misinforming, misleading, propelling hearts and lives out of control. Yet no one valuing health of mind and family life wants more of that.

So why, in the face of what we see, know, and suffer, do we accept this sickly mode of love? Why do we conform to the cult of modern consumer-romance?

Part of the reason, of course, is social habit. When everyone is taught to think and act the same, prevailing trends and lifestyles seem natural and normal, whatever they may be. People tend to sanctify the habitual.

A reason more difficult to face, perhaps, is our own unwell condition. Any society is, by definition, a group of people. Thus a sick society, by definition, is a group of sick people. As American theologian James I. Packer points out, "In moral and spiritual terms, we are all sick and damaged, scarred and sore, lame and lopsided, to a far, far greater extent than we realize." The ways of sickly love proceed from sickly hearts.

Finally, we lack ready alternatives. If we don't pursue the current form of ailing romance, what else can we do? How can we find effective love, satisfying love, enriching love, the kind of love that endures and ripples outward beneficially to everyone around us, then beyond us to future generations?

Many thoughtful and sensitive people today are questioning our way of loving, finding it wanting, and seeking something better. For them I suggest that we do not love enough, in the sense that we love only partially, incompletely. We accept fragmentary love as our standard. What we desperately need is a more complete, balanced, rounded love, a love that progresses to higher completion—a fuller, broadening, maturing, total love.

Part II

Love for Life

Love Rediscovered

THAT OUR AFFECTIONS KILL US NOT, NOR DYE.
—JOHN DONNE (1572–1631)

WHO CAN WE TURN TO?

O N THE SUBJECT OF LOVE, most media experts and other gurus have failed us abysmally. As long as they continue to lead us in the hopeless status quo and grope amid solutions that do not work, we have every reason to be wary of their guidance and to seek our own way.

But who, then, can we turn to? Rediscovering love, like reinventing our culture, is a process too vast, too complex, and too risky for any one person to attempt. So where can we go for reliable counsel? How can we find our way to effective love?

I propose that we start with the wisdom of other times and places. We can reach back two thousand years and more and find understandings sounder than our own. Then we can add experiences from our lives, yours and mine. Finally, we can call upon our own common sense, which experts have talked us out of so completely that this natural perception available to anyone seems hardly common anymore.

Combining timeless wisdom with what we see around us and what we sense within ourselves, we can see how to love and be loved in ways that benefit rather than harm or destroy.

THREE LOVES

Part of the reason love is lost in confusion is semantic. The little, single-syllable word is assigned far too much weight. It cannot bear all the burdens of meaning that our language expects it to carry. Overworked to the point of incoherence, it leads us only to bewilderment.

"Love," in our time, cries out for definition. Yet we find only confused garble. We can do better if we turn to the ancient Greeks, the master psychologists of their day and probably of all time.

Around 400 BC, the philosopher Socrates observed, "one part of love is separated off and receives the name of the whole. . . ." That is exactly our semantic problem. We isolate romance from other kinds of love then behave as though no other kinds of love existed.

Yet love is broader than romance—enormously so! As Socrates implied, the word has more than one meaning. It follows that each meaning leads to different actions and results.

Ancient Greeks recognized the diversity of love by using several words to describe it. Their terms might strike us as stiff and alien, sounding altogether too Greek to our ears. Yet I shall use three of them anyway, because our modern language offers no clear equivalents.

The first form of love in their basic three-part definition they called *eros*. This also was the name of the Greek god of love. Eros generally represents the urgent desire every person feels for self-fulfillment, the longing that leads us to reach out for something to make ourselves more complete. Eros says I want, I need—therefore I love. In that sense, it sounds like a pop song.

As eros focuses mainly on the self, the second kind of love begins to shift the spotlight to the wants and needs of others. *Philia* (from *philos*, or dear) represents brotherly love and intimate friendship—both, however, at a depth not common in our culture, where brothers do not necessarily love one another and friendships usually are shallower than philia implies.

With philia, the object of love becomes important in its own right, not merely something to be used but someone valued for his or her own sake. True friends promote each other's separate welfare as their own. This kind of love emphasizes not only getting but also giving.

The third major form of love identified by the Greeks is *agape* (pronounced ah-gáh-pay or ág-ah-pay), which proceeds even further. This is pure giving-love. It is expressed in generous service rendered solely to aid the life of someone or something else. No strings are attached. No return is expected. Theologically, agape is God's love for his creation. On the human plane, it can be compared to the love of an emotionally healthy mother for her baby, which she gives with no regard for what the baby can do for her in return.

Ancient Romans also recognized these three forms of love, naming them in Latin *amor, amicitia,* and *caritas.*

APPLYING THREE LOVES

The Greek categories of these three different kinds of love help us to understand a broader range of love than we are used to. At that point a new question arises: How are we to apply love's divisions? Are we to beam different kinds of love toward different objects, tailoring our love for each situation: eros for romance, philia for friendships, agape for babies and beggars? Does the system suggest three different love-roles, three activities, each separate and mutually exclusive?

To some extent it does. From moment to moment and deed to deed, we can switch from one kind of love to another simply by choosing to do so. We can shift from eros to philia to agape by a deliberate act of will.

For the longer term, though, we cannot make the switch as readily. Within each of us, one or another of these kinds of love predominates. That one mainly rules our emotions, leads us from our heart. This is because the three loves are not just different kinds. They also represent different levels. They are love at successive stages of spiritual-emotional growth. They are steps toward maturity.

The Greeks didn't tell us that, so far as I know. Nor have modern psychologists, at least not clearly. But we do not need anyone to tell us. We can see it for ourselves. We can watch the three kinds of love unfolding as human beings mature in their emotional life.

Eros is love at the beginner's level. I want, I need, gimmie-gimmie what I cry for, and I will dote on you in return. This is love as we see infants doing it—baby-love, consumer-love, a love that seeks personal gratification. People at the early stages of emotional maturity—whether small or tall—habitually hunger, crave, long to suckle and be filled, then gurgle with delight when they feel satisfied. It is not without significance that modern romancers call each other "baby" and baby-talk has been known as romance's special language of affection.

Researchers have discovered that the less emotionally mature a person is, the deeper he or she falls into this kind of love. People who are emotionally retarded to the point of illness and live in a super-hungry, womb-state condition of negative maturity fall the hardest.

As we see in our society every day, love cannot grow solely from desperate wanting or even gratitude for things supplied. When it ends with these emotions it is doomed to decay in unfulfillment. Love requires more if it is to survive.

Philia is more. You can see this second stage of love operating in children from about the age of five onward. They instinctively sense the principle of giving as well as getting—of fairness. "It's not fair," they'll protest if benefits seem out of balance. Philia is the love natural to their level of emotional maturity: a swap-love hinging on justice, an interplay of rights and duties, a harmony of self-seeking and self-giving. Psychologists tell us that most wedded couples whose marriages endure have succeeded in moving from eros up to this level of love.

Agape—no-strings-attached giving—is more still of what makes love thrive. But who does that? Major religions say we all should do it. Many saints the world over have been revered for success in agape. Good neighbors, peacemakers, humanitarians, philanthropists, people of persistent kindness and indomitable good will all aim at agape. And the more they aim, the more they attain, gradually growing in their emotional-spiritual being, in maturity, in their ability to achieve it.

The problem of love's definition, then, is not entirely semantic but springs as well from differences in emotional maturity. The meaning of the word shifts with each individual speaker. It rises on an ascending scale of connotation, with desperate craving at the lowest end of eros and the most selfless giving at the highest end of agape. The meaning varies according to the emotional growth, or development, or maturity, of each and every person who uses the word "love."

With the levels of love arranged on this ascending scale, "love" begins to make sense. Eros and agape lie at opposite ends. Love begins its existence as an infant hungry to consume, and rises to the munificence of high maturity. Consumer-love and producer-love seem opposites, both in the behavior they inspire and in the level of emotional maturity achieved by the lovers who practice them. Yet they both are fully valid love, connected on the long continuum of the rising scale.

This ascending scale is a key to understanding the otherwise impossibly bewildering phenomenon of love. It also can help us in our personal lives to make our way to effective, humanly beneficial, and lasting love.

"REAL" LOVE

In our time, many people argue about which kind of love is "real" or "true" and which is not. Some specialists, including psychologists Theodor Reik and Dorothy Tennov, recoil from the greedy grabbing of modern consumer-romance and declare that eros, with its insatiable hungers, should be thought of not as love but as something else, like Tennov's "limerence." Some altruistic thinkers deny the name "love" even to philia. The Indian spiritual leader Mahatma Gandhi considered a relationship that wants to get as much as to give to be not love but commerce. Psychologist Erich Fromm and sociologist Pitirim Sorokin regarded only altruism—as in the acts of agape—worthy of being called real love.

Sigmund Freud, on the other hand, said all these things fit under the same broad word, be it "love" in English or "*liebe*" in his native German. And so they do, when we see the three basic loves of the Greeks on an ascending scale.

Then the endlessly asked question, "Is it infatuation or love?" is rightly answered by saying: "It's both, they're no different, they're one in the same—on the level of eros." And what of puppy love? What about a crush? They are valid love, too—also eros.

Some years ago, women's magazines were preaching marriage as a fifty-fifty proposition. This is love on the level of philia, in which partners are caring, respectful, and considerate, yet also protective of their personal rights.

A few tender relationships, however rare they might be, reflect the love that the Apostle Paul described to Christians of the ancient Greek city of Corinth when he said love is patient, kind, not jealous, not putting on airs, never rude, not self-seeking, not prone to anger, not brooding over injuries, endlessly forebearing, trusting, hoping, enduring, never failing. That is agape at its own higher reaches.

So how can I tell if I'm in love? Which is "real" love, "true" love, "genuine" love, "authentic" love? They all are real, true, genuine, and authentic—at different levels of emotional growth and maturity. And, of course, they all have different consequences.

"I think I know what real love is," declared thirty-five-year-old Keith R., a stockbroker from Beverly Hills, California. Traveling to Washington, D.C., to pursue a twenty-year-old woman he met in a shoe store, he spent six days and $20,000 plying her with caviar and champagne, musicians and clowns, while he kept a limousine and a Lear Jet waiting in the hope she would marry him and fly away to Europe. His "real" love of that moment was eros. Her response: "I'm not in the mood to get married."

Robynne C., in her opinion, discovered real love by contrasting her feelings of the moment with past relationships. An American, she became engaged to Ian F., a Briton, after three million words exchanged electronically on the Internet. She was quoted by the *Observer* newspaper of London: "At first I felt stupid. But although I have been engaged and have had many relationships in which I thought I was in love, this relationship is so profound I now realize I was never in love before." Yet of course she was in love before—in eros love, which ebbs and flows, comes and goes, rises like a fever then dissipates all by itself. In each case, Mr. Right actually was Mr. Right Now.

Confusion over philia is expressed in this letter to a newspaper advice columnist:

> I'm married to a wonderful man. He is very generous, hardworking, and has always earned a decent living for us. He provides me with a new car and a lovely home. Everyone thinks I have the ideal husband and thinks he is a terrific

guy—including me. The only problem is that although we have always gotten along and I have always been proud to call him my husband, I'm not sure I ever really loved him. How important is it to be in love with the man you are married to when everything else is so good? [signed] Not In Love But Living Well

Does this writer, who seems to have missed the thrills of eros, love her husband? Probably she does, at the philia level, and he perhaps loves her even more. It is easy to overlook this calm but reliable and lasting love amid the barrage of messages from the society inducing us to stay at love's beginning—in baby-love, consumer-love, pleasure-love—all our days.

And what of agape? Take the case of Otto Springer, a German living in Prague during World War II. Springer worked as the Nazi-appointed "Aryan" head of a Jewish-owned company. Offered a transfer to Asia, where he could have lived in security, he remained in Czechoslovakia helping Jews avoid Nazi persecution. He protected his employees, forged false documents for Jews, and bribed Gestapo officials and guards in concentration camps. Ultimately he was sentenced to a concentration camp himself. There he continued helping people. Springer's care for his fellow human beings is classic agape—the highest, most heroic, most sacrificial love of all.

Though we can separate love's three basic levels as distinct categories in our minds, in daily life they mix and merge. Sometimes they exist in a pure state for a season. Eros-love especially often persists in unmixed form for weeks, months, occasionally years. More often, however, the three levels of love shift and blend within us. They can change their balance moment by moment.

Few eros-lovers like to be "baby" all the time. The passivity of passion, the feebleness of endless wanting and needing, the anxiety of dependence feel wearying and uncomfortably precarious if sustained too long. Meanwhile, philia's deep and devoted friendship can shift back to eros at times. When love and the lover are growing healthily, both eros and philia also drive them forward more and more into the realm of agape. Also, no doubt, even the most devoted agape in its noble self-forgetting must occasionally slip backward to philia for comfort, rest, and relief.

The three kinds of love can mingle and merge until we hardly can distinguish one from another. Yet it helps us in our lives to keep the three loves distinct in our minds. A clear awareness of love's three levels provides us with a plan for our personal progress, a map leading to our growth into total love.

Eros Aglow

IN EVERYTHING CONCERNING LOVE THERE IS
A NEED FOR FAR MORE CLARITY, HONESTY, IDEALISM. . . .
—ISAK DINESEN (1885–1962)

WISE PEOPLE of ancient and modern times have stood in awe before the power and glory of eros. Hebrew peoples called it *ahawa*, from the root "to glow." Socrates proclaimed, "Human nature will not easily find a helper better than [eros] love." Plato called eros "the greatest of heaven's blessings" and considered it the major source of human motivation. Other thinkers have defined this kind of love as a natural longing for the beautiful. The English poet W. H. Auden called it "builder of cities." Some philosophers have seen in eros the impetus for the rise and growth of civilizations.

All this might seem to us a bit too much credit for the erotic. But here again we are limited by semantics, by cultural understanding, and by habits of love that take the glow, the glory, and the might out of eros and diminish it to mere sensual thrills.

In the emotionally degraded society of the present, eros usually denotes little more than sexual titillation. Yet for the Greeks who invented the word and carefully defined the phenomenon, eros was not simple lust. They used another word—*epithymia*—for that. Meanwhile, their eros ranged far beyond mere sexuality. It included libido but also transcended it in a many-splendored way, denoting not only the motive for sex but also its meaning.

Epithymia, or sexual desire, is a fact about ourselves. We wholly misuse "erotic" when we apply the word to that. In its accurate sense, eros is far more about the beloved. While the sex-urge pushes from the inside, eros draws us from the outside. Raw lust hungers for the thrust of sex, for sensory pleasure or relief, turning the other person into hardly more than an apparatus for the job. Eros-love, on the other hand, yearns for the entire person of the beloved rather than for any specific pleasure that might be exacted. Lust, once satisfied, self-destructs. Eros, brimming with the best of romance, saves sex from such cold and brutal annihilation.

EROS AS LIFE FORCE

Yet even that is not all there is to eros, but only a good beginning. Eros, in its fuller workings, acts upon us constantly, spurring us onward and upward in many aspects of our lives.

Eros on the level of romance is the drive of love to unite and procreate. But its more complete definition involves humankind's longing for creative fulfillment. Eros leads us to transcend our present selves. It urges us toward union with our potential, to be all we can be, even as we seek fulfillment through other people and things. It inspires us with yearning for wholeness and meaning. It animates our longing to reach out, to grow and expand. Eros drives us forward toward the realm of new possibilities, fresh goals, loftier ideals.

Eros leads the intelligent to seek knowledge, the wise to strive toward a personal union with truth. It turns adventurers into explorers, dreamers into poets, inquirers into inventors and scientists. Its yearnings motivate the finest human beings to dedicate themselves to cultivating goodness and nobility. Eros is the force that generates within us tensions to blend, unite, bind, and build. It is part of the life instinct calling for life to continue, increase, and thrive.

Nor is even that the end of eros. At a still more exalted level eros has been seen as the spirit that created all life on earth. Eros, after all, was a god to the ancient Greeks.

Their mythology relates that in the beginning the world lay silent and barren. Then the god Eros appeared carrying a sheaf of life-giving arrows. He shot them one by one at the bleak, cold ground. As they pierced dead crust, the earth burst forth in luxuriant vegetation. Soon the world was abounding with life, animation, and joy. Then Eros took clay and shaped man and woman. He breathed into their nostrils the spirit of life. Thus did Eros bring the living world into being.

The psychologist Carl Gustav Jung said we cannot understand the phenomenon of eros unless we also fathom its divine significance. The theologian St. Augustine, bishop of the North African city of Hippo in the last days of the Roman Empire, pursued the same idea when he thought of eros as the yearning for mystical union with God.

The Bible's eighty-first Psalm says, "I am the Lord your God, who brought you up out of the land of Egypt. Open your mouth wide, and I will fill it." In Judeo-Christian tradition, the Creator plants the need-love of eros within us so we will turn to him for what we need, as well as to each other. Eros, as the appetite for self-fulfillment, thus can focus on God for satisfaction of spiritual hunger by joyously attaining and partaking of divine perfections.

THE LOOK OF LOVE

The course of true romance, in a general way, tends to run the same for everyone. The traits of eros-love are predictably constant, as regular as the rising of the sun. See one romance and you've seen them all. Even their future unfolding is predictable:

✦ Eros-lovers are ready for love before it happens. Their availability can take many forms: questing for adventure, wanting to leave home, suffering from loneliness, cut off in a strange place, longing to love and be loved, psychologically or financially prepared to make a life-time commitment. Some prospective lovers love to be in love. The nineteenth-century French novelist Stendhal was infatuated most of his life with one woman or another, claiming that romantic love, no matter how distressing or how much it turned one into a fool, was unrivaled for the zest it brought to human existence. The twentieth-century American dancer Isadora Duncan wrote in her diary when she was in her mid-thirties that after her initial experience with romance she was continually in love.

+ Eros-lovers are endlessly optimistic. It seems odd that anyone should waltz eagerly into a venture we all know to be enormously costly in time and energy, to be boobytrapped with illusions, to commonly cause great pain and sometimes despoil lives. Yet even as lovers face such huge cost and precarious promise, they invariably remain drunk on hope. Romance is one of the few endeavors where people rarely learn much from experience.

+ An eros-lover might approach romance freely, but the emotions of the experience quickly turn compulsive and obsessive. In no time eros-love takes over the lover's life, reorganizing and often disrupting it. This is not necessarily pleasant. It can hinder studies, work, and other vital concerns, which suddenly seem less important. Some eros-lovers invest their whole existence in their beloved.

+ Eros strikes like a sudden invader. Seekers after sex alone pick partners consciously and voluntarily. Not so eros-lovers, who feel they did not select each other coolly and sensibly but were hurled together by fate, destiny, passion, or heaven itself. "Love is like a fever that comes and goes quite independently of the will," said Stendhal. Its fixations are not free but impelled. Eros is passive, as the word "passion" implies in its root meaning: being acted upon.

+ Early romancers often are nervous, shy, awkward, tongue-tied, confused, flushed, pale, and unusually excited. Researchers have detected distinct physical symptoms of romance: palpitations of the heart, rapid breathing, flushing of the face, and slight tremor of hands or fingers. A shot of adrenaline can create the same effects.

+ First-romancers believe their love is an experience of a lifetime, one of a kind, unknowable to their elders, unprecedented in history. All earnest romancers feel their love is rare and uniquely deep, intense, and strong.

+ Eros-lovers usually know when they fell in love, but rarely can they say why. Love pierced them like an arrow from Cupid's bow, infused them like a potion, came upon them like a sorcerer's enchantment. Eros, with its irrational force, sometimes brings together the most unsuitable people. Many predictably unhappy marriages begin with this blindest kind of love.

✦ Unlike seekers after sex, who can shift readily from one connection to another, true romancers can be in love with only one person at a time, except near the beginning or the end of a relationship.

✦ Eros-lovers endow their partners with a "halo effect." A few highly admired traits of the beloved are emphasized, while imperfections go unnoticed or ignored. Stendhal described this as "a mental process which draws from everything that happens new proofs of the perfection of the loved one." As the actor John Barrymore ungallantly put it, "Love is the delightful interval between meeting a girl and discovering that she looks like a haddock."

✦ A major symptom of romance is illusion. One of the definitions of the word "romance" is "fantasy." The lover sees his damsel, and she her knight, with strange intensity, as someone of extraordinary excellence. With the wave of love's wand, perfectly ordinary girls and boys are transformed into near-divinities endowed with exquisite beauty, fascinating personality, admirable character. "Love is a human religion," observed psychologist Robert Seidenberg, "in which another person is believed in."

✦ Eros-lovers are delighted and preoccupied with each other. While their attraction might be triggered by beauty, wealth, status, or sexual feelings, seldom does any one factor serve as a prime focus. The romancer is entranced with the beloved's total person—at least as she or he is imagined to be. Plagued by what anthropologist Helen Fisher calls "intrusive thinking," the lover ponders this being of great wonder uncontrollably, hour after hour, day and night.

✦ Some psychologists believe that eros-lovers are dissatisfied with themselves and project on the other person qualities they would like to possess. They read a partner like a Rorschach ink blot test. They hallucinate what they want to see. The Italian Renaissance sculptor, painter, and poet Michelangelo wrote a sonnet comparing a beloved woman to a block of marble from which the lover sculpts the statue of his dreams. In Greek mythology King Pygmalion of Cyprus did just that. He carved an ivory statue of a woman, fell in love with the image, then prayed to Aphrodite, mother of Eros and goddess of love, to give it life. Transformed, the statue became his wife, Galatea.

✦ Since eros-love rarely involves real human beings but only idealized images, a romantic lover is not likely to become captivated by someone he or she knows well. Acquaintances work better and strangers best. A considerable degree of unfamiliarity is useful for illusions to be conjured up and sustained.

✦ Though some eros-lovers enjoy being glorified, others feel their pedestal as an uncomfortably precarious perch. The love object might feel unable to live up to such extravagant expectations and fear becoming a source of disappointment.

✦ As eros-love grows, so do its desires, rising to heights of impetuous intensity. Romancers are racked with longing—though not, as modern fiction would have it, for sex. Rarely is sex the principal focus of true romance and never can sex alone satisfy its desires. Sexual urges and thoughts might even feel inappropriate, disrespectful, a defilement of the celestial object. Eros-love wants more than physical fusion. It desires to be with, contemplate, and adore the beloved constantly.

✦ Eros yearns more than anything else to be loved in return. As psychologist Dorothy Tennov points out, the eros-lover cannot rest until assured of reciprocation. That, not sex, is the goal of true romance. The French painter Henri de Toulouse-Lautrec observed this when he said, "Love is a disease that fills you with a desire to be desired." Only when eros is answered with eros can lovers soar to heights of blissful ecstasy. But timing is important here. It pays to play it cool. If an "I love you" comes too quickly, too easily, a partner might get nervous or lose interest and drift away.

✦ As Tennov also cites, eros as an emotional high needs insecurity to survive. Sensing the danger in declaring affections too soon, lovers rarely dare to be frank, open, and sincere about their feelings. Some accomplished romancers play games, manipulate, withhold, and deceive to hone a razor-edge of uncertainty. A romance as confusing as a maze of mirrors only serves to whet the appetites of eros. When, on the other hand, uncertainty is removed, even by longed-for reciprocation, desires begin to relax and cool. The need for uncertainty also explains why some romancers fall in love with unattainable people, whether married, far away, or distanced by other obstacles. Uncertainty can keep romance at fever pitch for years—as long as one more vital emotion is present.

✦ Hope is as important to eros-love as uncertainty. As Socrates noted in ancient Greece, Ovid in ancient Rome, the *Kama Sutra* in ancient India, and Dear Abby and Dorothy Tennov in current times, uncertainty and hope both are essential ingredients of eros. One plays off the other. They teeter in delicate balance: first uncertainty, then hope, then doubt soothed by assurance, then uncertainty again and more seeking after hope. If hope dies utterly, so does romance, suddenly and absolutely. That implies that the kindest end to a romance is a clean, clear, unequivocal, indisputable break.

✦ While eros-love seeks fulfillment in reciprocation, it does not necessarily aim for pleasure or happiness. Eros thrives on adversity—an aspect of the insecurity it needs. It faces obstacles with determination and perseverance. A challenge like parental objections can fan eros-love to seething heat. Try to persuade lovers that their marriage will be difficult, even unhappy, and they might believe you but they will not separate. They might even face death, as legendary lovers have done, provided they can face it together. Eros-lovers are prepared for any loss except being parted.

✦ A principal value of modern romance is ego affirmation. As much as romancers feel full of want and need, they also long to be wanted, needed, valued, accepted. The three little words "I love you" need not signify a promise of service, loyalty, or anything else requiring effort, sacrifice, or benefit. The words are sufficient in themselves to bolster the ego of a romancer full of self-doubt, no matter how fragile and temporary the affirmation is likely to be.

✦ When romance is running smoothly, lovers often feel buoyant, as though walking on air. They also might feel a tingling in the region of the heart. When things are going poorly, they suffer aching in the chest or an emptiness or hollowness in the abdominal region. The physiology of eros also goes to the head. Some scientists link the euphoria of infatuation to brain chemicals called monoamines. If romancers rise on the ascending scale of love to the more comfortable affection of philia, eros-love calms and morphine-like substances called endorphins come into play.

✦ Eros-lovers suddenly find themselves loving life and the world and everything in it. "From the very first moment he looked into my eyes," a young woman related, "I had this strangely blissful feeling like nothing I'd ever felt before. All my problems and troubles became unimportant. I saw them from afar, separated by an ocean of pure happiness. My car had broken down and my credit was maxed out. I didn't care! I was his and he was mine. That was all that mattered. Life was wonderful. The trees were greener, the sky bluer, the sun caressed my face. I beamed at the world, greeted everyone I saw and the world beamed back at me. I could hardly keep from shouting how ecstatically happy I was. I longed to share my joy with everyone."

Perhaps the splendid new existence that eros promises is a genuine foretaste of what life can become if we do not end our loving with eros but ascend to love's loftier levels. Is eros-love a vision of heaven where love completes its full potential? Or is it, as some dour critics say, a trick of nature to bring self-absorbed people together long enough to breed and keep the human race going? It might be either, the choice being our own.

If we rise above preoccupation with personal desires and cease seeing our partner mainly as a means to self-fulfillment, we can answer the question, "Is there love after romance?" in the affirmative. If we focus more of our attention on the welfare of our beloved, giving and serving with active care, generosity, and kindness, this exercise in the ways of higher love will have the strengthening effects of any exercise. Loving generously will bring us upward to higher levels of loving, delivering us ever-nearer to the highest goal of total love.

If, on the other hand, we stop at romance's thrills and pleasures and do little to expand our generosity, we will see our love disintegrate and possibly turn grotesque and ugly.

Eros Awry

ALL'S FAIR IN LOVE AND WAR.
—F. E. SMEDLEY (1818–1864)

EROS IS A NATURAL FREEBIE, bliss on the house. But we receive it only for a limited time. Remember Tristan and Isolde's three-year love potion? And Dorothy Tennov's "average limerent duration" of approximately two years? That's about all the lyrical enchantment anyone can expect from romance.

Eros gives us enough emotional fuel to get us going in love. It primes our emotional pump. It draws couples together and makes the start of love easy. But that's all it does. It is a fund for investment, rather than an endless bonanza to be squandered on pleasure.

Pop songs promising everlasting romantic bliss are a fiction. Eros is fickle by nature, the most fragile and perishable of all the forms of love. It is brought on by attraction, allure, seduction. Loss or diminishment of that appeal turns it off again. More compelling attraction somewhere else induces it to stray.

Its solemn vows pledging faithfulness for all eternity might be sworn in utter sincerity with intense and earnest feeling. Yet the ardent assurances of eros in the end are no more than sweet nothings. This is because eros promises what it cannot give. It holds out as a guarantee what really is no more than an opportunity.

To think of love mainly as fevered emotion and then expect it will last is a contradiction in terms. Feelings never last. They rise and fall, wax and wane, come and go. Emotion tells us only of the moment. That's what emotion is for. It is our here-and-now detector, our inner sensor proclaiming present well-being or distress.

Emotion has little memory and less foresight. We cannot recall fully the thrill of a roller coaster ride, the savor of a steak, the delicate delight of a first kiss. Not even the terror of trauma can be re-evoked just as it happened without pathologically reliving it. We can use our intellect to recall remnants of the past and to predict things to come. Intellect is our time-traveler. But emotion is virtually useless for forecasting the future. Feelings speak only of the moment.

So present-day romancers who expect eros-love to endure like some eternal nirvana are in danger of burning their tanks of emotional fuel on a joyride to nowhere. They squander what should be their investment fund on euphoria. They visit love like a free-lunch counter, play it like a lottery without buying a ticket, and ultimately end up with a fly-now, pay-later plan that leaves them bankrupt.

"Passion rarely lasts very long," say University of Wisconsin sociologists and love-researchers Elaine and G. William Walster. "Most passionate affairs end simply: the lovers find someone else they love more. A few affairs end tragically. The lovers start out intensely committed to one another, but, in time, their feelings change. Passionate love erupts into ambivalence or hatred. Only over a period of time do these intense emotions cool to bearable indifference."

As eros-love departs, its promises no longer feel binding. Romancers looking back on past relationships often feel foolish to have made such commitments. Many shudder to think what might have happened had they tuned the key of wedlock. Ex-lovers sometimes feel revolted by past relationships.

LOVE AND EVIL

"Is love evil?" I saw the question scrawled on a men's room wall in the small Hawaiian town of Hilo. Sophisticated thinking that seemed, for such a setting. Yet perhaps it was not thinking at all but a cry of raw emotion, a proposition cast in the logic of pain: Evil harms, love harmed me, therefore is love evil?

The answer, of course, is: Yes, love can be evil. Like the full range of total love on its ascending scale, eros at the lower end of the scale has levels of its own. At its heights it is healthy and creative. At its lower depths it becomes sickly and destructive. The levels of eros coincide with degrees of emotional health and illness. Though still called "love," and logically so, eros, as it nears the bottom of love's scale, often turns malignant and threatens havoc.

The ancient Greeks noted the variations within eros. Over the centuries of their culture, art shows the god Eros in three different forms. The diverse depictions reflect the emotional condition of the people in the culture's various ages: first in a healthy social order, then in a culture losing its way, finally in a society in decay.

Eros in his earliest form is shown as a beautiful winged youth— strong, handsome, bearded, the virile god of creativity. The later Eros is softer and more thoughtful. Finally he degenerates into an effete, rosy, dimpled, infantile Cupid, stunted and fat, never growing up—Baby Love making roguish mischief with the bow and arrows that once the god had used to bring life to the earth. Sometimes Eros was portrayed wearing armor like that of Mars, god of war, possibly suggesting links between love and combat.

When love turns malignant or evil, lower-level eros is the culprit. As a me-centered love on the beginner's level, eros offers us a chance to develop our love into something higher and finer. But if we do not grasp this chance, it degenerates in the opposite direction.

As eros is a desiring, a longing, an endless reaching for growth and stretching of self, it also is a mark of our incompleteness. Rooted in emotional and spiritual need, it is hungry and acquisitive by nature. If we fail to strive in romance toward generosity and higher maturity, then we invite descent into a sickly, symbiotic, parasitic, emotionally cannibalistic union. Low-level love pulls and tugs, sucks and feeds, looting for its emotional sustenance. In time, partners caught in sickly eros feel drained and must break apart for self-preservation and recuperation.

Eros at its finest brings out much that is good in us. Gone bad, it can exhume our absolute worst. With both a positive and a negative side, eros holds equal potential for creativity and destruction. Significantly, the earliest goddess of romantic love—Ishtar of the Summerian civilization—was also the goddess of war. Literature of the period describes her as equally vicious in both roles.

Freud called eros "the mischief maker." Plato warns in *The Symposium*, the first philosophical masterpiece on love, "Eros is a *daimon*." He does not mean demon as we interpret the word, a personified spirit of evil. Rather, the classical Greek daimon implies a natural function that can prove productive but just as readily turns evil and malevolent.

Thousands of years of history record the ravages of eros in the classic tales of Helen and Paris, Orpheus and Euridice, Tristan and Isolde, Antony and Cleopatra, Romeo and Juliet. Similar legends in scores of languages warn of the power of erotic love to sweep hapless lovers out of rational control and hurl them toward ruin and destruction.

Is love evil? Many of us have personally seen the might of eros as a blind, draining, disintegrative force.

Reflect on need-love, as Plato did, as "the son of Poverty," then consider that poverty delivers no gifts. Recall love as it destroys peace of mind with obsessive desires and involuntary passions. Suffer love as an exercise of power and control. Experience love as being suffocatingly possessed. Feel love as a dissolution of self into another. Hear lovers screaming and fighting in a terrifying persistence of nursery years. See lovers mercilessly devouring each other. Endure eros as unbearable, inescapable pain. Stand on the border between love and madness—"madly in love." Consider crimes of passion: assault, rape, suicide, murder, maniacal violence.

The ancients understood well the degeneration of eros into a disease. In a genealogy of the gods titled *Theogony*, written by the Greek farmer-poet Hesiod as early as the eighth century BC, Eros is a god who overcomes the reason both of mortals and of fellow gods. In the drama *Antigone*, written in the fifth century BC by the tragic poet Sophocles, Eros is described as unconquerable, inescapable, destructive, driving sound minds to insanity and good people to malevolence.

Along its downward course, eros disintegrates into strange perversions that nullify all benefits and leave only devastation. We read of two lovers in Japan leaping off a railway bridge to their death. A lover's quarrel in New York leads a forty-year-old man to dump gasoline around the entrance to a dance hall, incinerating twenty-five people. A twenty-nine-year-old security guard in East London, South Africa is jilted by his girl-friend and kills her and nine other people, wounds seven others, then turns the gun on himself. A photographer in Honolulu, in the wake of a failed marriage, feeds cyanide to his seven-year-old daughter then poisons himself. A Kansas minister and his secretary, falling in love and fearing divorce might harm his career, prepare to wed by murdering their spouses. A young woman in love with a man who does not want her two children locks the toddlers in a car and drowns them in a lake.

When such hearts go bumpity-bump, it's love, love, love, true enough —but eros gone awry. Eros-lovers in other social roles might be normal, rational, emotionally stable, socially functional people. But in love affairs, minds can churn and twist until romancers are as deranged as the certifiably insane.

Because of eros's penchant for mischief and menace, theologians and guardians of nubile youth traditionally have distrusted romantic love. While not always denouncing it as evil, they have recognized eros as potentially dangerous to wedlock, life, and the eternal soul.

Involuntary and uncontrollable, eros-love clashes with the fundamental Judeo-Christian tenet of free will. How can people surrendering to its compulsions remain unfettered, rational, responsible creatures of God? Religious thinkers in both ancient and modern times have seen eros as a form of idolatry, with lovers idolizing each other or eros itself.

To lovers, eros can seem a godlike thing transcending all else in life, worthy of total devotion. Its temptations constrain like duty. Its desires feel like commands. Resistance to the leadings of romance can seem unfaithful, whether it impels unchastity, injustice, unkindness, or criminality. Anything done in the name of love can feel justified, regardless of cost. With eros mistaken for a deity, the precept "God is love" is turned backwards to "Love is god."

Eros transformed into a religion leads its followers to seduce the innocent, betray spouses, abandon children, lie, cheat, steal, kill. In its misshapen form, romance might cut its swath of damage and die young. Or, as English writer C. S. Lewis describes, it might drag on, "mercilessly chaining together two mutual tormentors, each raw all over with the poison of hate-in-love, each ravenous to receive and implacably refusing to give, jealous, suspicious, resentful, struggling for the upper hand, determined to be free and to allow no freedom, living on 'scenes.'" Thus, Lewis adds, "The lovers' old hyperbole of 'eating' each other can come horribly near to the truth."

IS ROMANCE DYING?

For several generations, observers of life and love in our society—from anthropologist Margaret Mead to novelist Ernest Hemingway to Canadian prophet of the information age Marshall McLuhan—have been telling us that romantic love is obsolete.

Harvard sociologist Pitirim Sorokin linked the death of romance to a grand transformation presently sweeping over the whole of Western culture. In a ten-year study that Sorokin organized, an international team of scholars charted European societies over 2,500 years. Compiling enormous sums of data, Sorokin found a regular and predictable alternation through the centuries between two vastly different ways of life.

One of these cultural paradigms Sorokin called the "sensate" way of life. Sensate culture, which prevails at present, finds its truth, life, and pleasures mainly through the five senses. It favors an existence built upon materialism and comfort. At the same time, it tends to downgrade or reject the spiritual side of life.

The second paradigm Sorokin called "ideational." This mode of culture reigned in very ancient Greece, in early Rome, and in medieval times. The ideational view of life finds ultimate reality not something material to be grasped by the senses but a spiritual quality: Brahma, Tao, Nirvana, Yahweh, Almighty God. The main concerns of people in an ideational age are not comfort, pleasure, or happiness, not riches, power, status, or fame. Such values are regarded as threats to peace of mind and health of soul. Instead, ideational concerns involve good and evil, consciousness and conscience, the welfare of souls and salvation. People in an ideational culture live ascetically and morally firm. They revel in strength of character and hardihood.

Each of these cultural paradigms dawns as a fresh discovery and a new road to creativity. As it gradually matures over centuries, it tries to force out elements of the opposite paradigm and gain a monopoly for itself. Spiritual cultures edge out the material. Conversely, a material culture tries to edge out the spiritual side of life. The farther one or the other culture moves through its creative period, the more it eliminates its opposite paradigm. Eventually it goes too far, becoming too sensual or too spiritual for human life to tolerate.

Either culture form ripens like a fruit, becoming overripe and rotten in its late stages. At that point, the culture disintegrates and collapses. Then the pendulum swings the other way, and the opposite culture form arises freshly with new creative life.

Modern Western culture, Sorokin believed, has reached the end of a sensate period that began with the Renaissance. For some five centuries, Western culture has run a sensate course. It has fulfilled splendidly many creative possibilities in the fine arts, religion, and philosophy; in political forms, ethics, and law; in science, technology, economics, and social relationships. But now its energies are depleted and its loftiest aspirations are largely abandoned. The culture is slumping into fatigue, declining toward collapse. The current transformation of Western culture, Sorokin judged, amounts to a paradigm shift no less historically momentous than the fall of ancient sensate Rome.

In such a time of decline, the arts turn confused, gross, outrageous. Science, once healthy and constructive, calculates methods of destruction. Institutions become corrupt. Organizations grow decadent. Pleasures intensify until they jade and kill.

Romantic love thrives in a sensate culture. In its early stages, like the culture itself, it draws ideals from an ideational culture that came before. It is tempered by old disciplines, habits of character, religious and altruistic ethics. But as romance ripens along with the sensate culture that gave rise to it, both turn overripe and fall into decay apace. Sensate-style love turns ever more selfish, crude, carnal, raw, and injurious. Eventually, along with the decaying sensate culture as a whole, the deteriorated form of love burns itself out and is abandoned.

Romance as we practice it today seems hardly likely to survive. It debases love—which in its higher forms is founded upon mutual care and kindness—into crude self-interest, insatiable hunger, grappling for advantage, an infantile insistence upon having one's own way, a struggle for dominance.

Even psychologists who favor romance make no great claims for its benevolence. Roger Callahan writes: "Romantic love is *selfish* [italics his]! When it comes to an authentic romantic relationship, it is *your* pleasure, and *your* happiness that's the central base of emotion. Lots of people believe that real love is total selflessness and a generous concern for someone else is really at its root. As 'nice' as this may sound, it has nothing to do with romantic love. A selfless romantic love is absurd."

When lovers choose lovers for personal advantage, they first fall in love then automatically fall away from love. When seekers after love stop short of regular generous giving, they bar themselves from higher and enduring love.

When a lover persuades a partner to give up self-interest without giving up his own, eros becomes a betrayal. When lovers try to cut the time as short as possible between meeting and consummation, romance can only go flat. Where the first signs of discomfort become signals to break up, eros cannot develop. When people trifle casually with love, they defile its symbols, mock its substance, and make love meaningless.

People in a morally extinguished society cannot help but wage a war of all against all. They dare not relax their guard. Single or wed, they watch their backs, not trusting anyone with more than they can afford to lose. Only legal contracts drawn up for disengaged individuals that stipulate giving and receiving so much but no more bring peace of mind. In a society where love has grown so cold, how can healthy romance flourish or even exist?

Rescuing Romance

Whatever problems we know romance brings today, many of us still want it in our lives. Almost everyone in the Western world adores romance, even people who never experience it.

Some do not, after all. Though eros can blossom among all races and creeds, in sickness or in health, and at any age, some people have felt little or nothing of its pleasures and travails. They have no understanding of the tingling stomach, the pressures in the chest, the intrusive daydreaming, the longing for reciprocation, the need for exclusivity, or any of the ecstasies and sufferings romancers know well.

Psychologist Dorothy Tennov tells of a woman twice married, divorced, and sexually active who confessed to being utterly baffled by the emotional ardor of some of her partners. One psychotherapist attributed her steadiness of feeling to neurosis, confusing her all the more. Yet, Tennov says, her condition is no more pathological than it is unique. Some people are too blunted by past liaisons to work up any more emotional passions. Others are emotionally mature enough to love perfectly well without falling into eros at all.

Yet most people in the Western world remain convinced that eros is a golden experience and anyone who has not savored its sensations has missed one of life's greatest gifts. They pursue romance because everyone raves about it and they want to be sure they are not missing something important.

No harm in that—as long as harm is averted. And it can be. Eros-love is not undesirable in itself, but only as a loose and empty pastime where romancers become battered, worn, and jaded before lasting love can begin. Romance at its best can be rescued, if not for the society at large, then for any individual person willing to pay the price of growing, lasting love. This amounts to exercising qualities like self-control, integrity, kindness.

Romance, above all other forms of love, needs control. By its nature, it is imprudent, wild, senseless, enslaving. It needs constant chastening of motives and corrections of course, all based upon principles of generous care and concern that govern the higher stages of love.

Throughout history, community standards normally provided the controls that eros needed. Exceptions occurred only in aberrant times: as when Antony and Cleopatra, in Shakespeare's words, "kiss'd away Kingdoms," and our own age when we kiss off one another. Social restrictions on eros-love have ranged from reasonable to repulsive. They include religious censure, chaperons, tribal taboos, confining women or hiding them in veils, even mutilating genitals to discourage unchastity. Many societies still exert such controls. The Western world, meanwhile, with its own former restraints lost, can only experiment with new controls in the hope of averting the chaos of eros unleashed.

Former Communist East Germany, for example, tried for years to rid its society of romantic love, labeling it, among other things, "bourgeois trash." Politics, however, proved unequal to the task of tamping down hearts and the effort finally was abandoned. Lately in America and other Western lands, religious and hygienic groups have promoted education in sexual abstinence and led youth to sign pledges of chastity.

It seems unlikely, though, that organized controls will spread through Western society enough to provide the restraint eros needs. People who want sound love in their lives are better off preparing to go it alone than waiting for broad social reform.

For ancient Greeks, choosing passions responsibly, rather than being chosen by them, was the essence of virtue. That is more easily said than done regarding romance. But even while passions might pursue paths of their own, we still can consciously govern our day-to-day attitudes and behavior.

Control begins with understanding the obvious: that eros-love is never enough love. Natural for many, unavoidable for some, it nonetheless is neither self-sufficient nor self-sustaining. Potentially as glorious as a garden of flowers, it remains, like a flower garden, fragile and perishable. Neglected, it either withers or is taken over by weeds.

Eros, if it is to keep its beauty, must be nurtured, pruned, and fenced. It must be nourished with kindness, fertilized with truthfulness, trimmed free of injustice, weeded of ill-feelings and selfishness, hedged with decency and self-denial, and exposed to the warmth of humane values and virtues. For romance to remain sweet, it must be ruled by consideration, fairness, and honesty.

These imperatives ring like a chorus through the words of love's great thinkers: The Christian theologian St. Augustine knew eros well from his own younger years, when he prayed, "Lord, give me chastity, but not yet." In his own time of romance, as the Roman Empire was collapsing, he advised that eros's tendencies, though fully natural, must be carefully guided by knowledge, kept under control, and combined with virtue.

The modern Christian writer C. S. Lewis also allowed eros a legitimate place in the scheme of love. Yet he warned against obeying its promptings fully, "for Eros, honoured without reservation and obeyed unconditionally, becomes a demon."

Psychologists Theodor Reik and Eric Fromm and philosopher José Ortega y Gasset affirm that acquisitive desire must be tempered with benevolence to keep love healthy and alive.

Psychologist Rollo May adds: "The erotic impulses can and should have some discipline: the gospel of the free expression of every impulse disperses experience like a river with no banks, its water spilled and wasted as it flows in every direction. The disciplining of eros provides *forms* in which we can develop and which protect us from unbearable anxiety. Freud believed that the disciplining of eros was necessary for civilized culture, and that it was from the repression and sublimation of erotic impulses that the power came out from which civilizations were built."

Philosopher of love Denis de Rougement writes: ". . . without the sexual discipline which the so-called puritanical tendencies have imposed upon us since Europe first existed, there would be nothing more in our civilization than in those nations known as underdeveloped, and no doubt less: there would be neither work, nor organized effort nor the technology which has created the present world."

Theodor Reik, who saw romance as a "phantom" and a "dream," also saw it as an opportunity for a more enduring form of love: "A new kind of companionship, different from romance but no less valuable, may result in a sense of ease and harmony. Although idealization has ceased and passion is gone, yet the atmosphere is clear and calm. The lover has changed into a friend. . . . Romance can disappear and evaporate, but something else can stay."

Eros at its best is a way to higher love. It is a prelude to enduring love, a sudden and magnificent chance to cast aside solitary concerns, to overleap selfishness, to make desire itself altruistic, to yield to spontaneous and effortless loving of another as oneself. As an image and a foretaste of greater love, eros is rich with the joys that may be gained if, on the wings of love, we rise beyond romance to total love.

The Cozy Love

A LITTLE-KNOWN LOVE

WHEN WE SPEAK of romantic love we find listeners attentive, interested, and well informed. They are thoroughly convinced of its importance in their lives. They know they need someone to fill their emptiness, and eros-level, me-centered, beginner's love promises to do this—however often the promise might be broken.

When we speak of the next higher level of love, few people of our time have any accurate idea of what we are talking about. Peoples of other periods in history considered *philia*—or deep friendship, or middle-level, we-centered love—the happiest and finest love of all. For them it was one of life's greatest blessings, the school of virtue, a pathway to higher humanity.

Said Aristotle, "No one would choose to live without friends." Said Socrates, "He who throws away a friend is as foolish as he who throws away his life." People in medieval times thought of friendship-love as holy. Ralph Waldo Emerson claimed that a human friend "may well be reckoned the masterpiece of nature."

We overlook this level of love. Today few people rank friendship anywhere near eros in value. Generally we don't consider it a form of love at all. "Let's just be friends," we say when we would rather not become involved in eros-love.

We concede that we need friends. Some people claim to have lots of them. Yet the word often carries little depth of meaning. Modern friendships tend to lack the open self-revelation, heartfelt intimacy, and unselfish mutual concern that in other times elevated friendship to lofty status.

In our age of haste and ambition, we feel too busy for deep friendships. Rushing to work, to meetings, to entertainments, we find little time to cultivate more than bland human contacts. We are far too preoccupied with fulfilling obligations and climbing the ladder of success to go to the trouble of cultivating real friends. We prefer in odd free moments to flop down and watch television. Many people today also feel too defensive to open their minds and hearts for the necessary intimacy of profound friendship. Self-exposure seems dangerous in a world of dogs eating dogs.

It seems easier to bypass this part of human existence that, after all, is not essential to our lives. However great the benefits of deep camaraderie, people can get along without it in the same way they can survive without philosophy or art.

And what if we did form a close friendship-bond, man to man, woman to woman, or for that matter woman to man? In a society simmering in carnality, observers would imagine that sex must be part of the mix, overtly, covertly, or repressed. Any intimate relationship is suspect. A close and frequent bond between people of one gender is automatically interpreted as homosexual. If sexual acts are absent between two companions, then homo-motives must be subconscious. Such suspicions cannot be proved, of course, but they cannot be refuted either.

All of these drawbacks leave only disconnected, mild friendships practical, socially safe, and prudent.

WHAT IS A FRIEND?

Our suspicions about friendship reflect our poverty in this level of love. Since few modern people have any understanding at all of philia—which probably is why we value it so little—most of us sadly pass through our adult lives without having any deep friends.

Yet we are not totally unfamiliar with close friendship and its joys. Once upon a time many of us knew it well. Psychologist John Bradshaw, who has examined the dysfunctions of modern love, tells of seeing an old photo of himself and three friends when he was about eleven years old. They are standing with arms draped over each other's shoulders. "There was a wonderful sense of safety in being the four musketeers," he writes. "And those were the days of some real joy in my childhood." Then he laments, "I've never *ever* recaptured the camaraderie and the spirit of friendship that I experienced then."

Psychologist Harry Stack Sullivan noted the "chum" stage in human development, from ages around eight to twelve, before heterosexual interests emerge. In those years, youngsters happily appreciate and vastly enjoy friends of their own gender. Boys commonly walk down the street with arms around one another's necks. Girls become inseparable companions. This is the natural beginning of the human capacity to care for someone else without immediate reference to oneself.

As eros seeks gain for self-fulfillment, philia also seeks to fulfill a companion's needs. As eros is baby-love, philia is child-love, natural to the child's level of emotional development. That's why children grasp its principle intuitively, incessantly talking of the need for fairness. As eros strives to get, philia exchanges, aiming toward equity, more or less equal, self-seeking and self-giving.

Philia, like eros and the total range of love, has its own ascending scale. Aristotle, discussing friendship in his *Nicomachean Ethics* notes three levels. The lowest form of friendship, a bare notch above eros, amounts to people consenting to use one another for personal advantage. Modern people understand that well. They use friends to get job leads, wholesale prices, or free baseball tickets. Other useful friends are people we can depend upon for help in time of need, which is kindness on their part though utilitarian on ours.

With low-level philia, giving is consciously rationed. Such a relationship can resemble a business contract in the classic ancient Roman formula: "Give to be given, serve to be served, give to be served, serve to be given." Justice is strict, going equally two ways. For the giver, any offering is less a gift than an investment. It implies obligation—"I owe you one."

Aristotle also described such an alliance as pseudo-friendship, in which one loves "not in so far as the friend *is* but only in so far as she or he is useful or pleasurable. Such a friendship, of course, is very liable to dissolution when it is no longer pleasurable." Its parties remain separate, never blending into a unified "we."

Aristotle's second level of friendship brings people together to do things and enjoy each other's company. Our culture understands that, too. Friends like this fill some of our hours with distraction, amusement, or purpose. They come to dinner, join us at the theater, shop with us in the mall. They are hunting companions, drinking buddies, business associates, lodge fellows, club members, allies in one cause or another. With them we are congenial, bluff, hearty. Yet here again, relationships often lack depth and unreserved confidence.

Aristotle's highest level of friendship is least common among us: a comradeship of mutual concern and active care. Here friends lead and inspire each other, not merely supporting one another as they are but helping to bring out and develop each other's finest qualities.

Aristotle saw philia as an extension of self-love, with the friend felt as similar to the self—a sort of second self whose welfare is important in its own right. "We may describe friendly feelings toward anyone," he explained, "as wishing for him what we believe to be good things, not for your sake but for him, and trying your best to bring these things about."

The thirteenth-century theological philosopher Thomas Aquinas added, ". . . not every love has the character of friendship, but that love that is together with benevolence, that is, we love someone so as to wish him well. . . ." Aquinas also said: ". . . the happy man needs friends, not indeed to make use of them, since he suffices himself, not to delight in them since he possesses perfect delight in the operation of virtue, but so that he may do them good, that he may delight in seeing them do good, and again that he may be helped in his good work by them. For in order that man may do well, whether in the works of active life, or in those of contemplative life, he needs the fellowship of friends." Friendship at its best, medieval people believed, could elevate human beings to the level of angels.

Philia also can develop in a negative direction. Some deep friendships also are deeply perverse. A crime syndicate or a street gang can forge an accepting, loving, familial fellowship that grants mutual support for thievery, murder, rape, and all manner of corruption. Individual members might shrink from such evils when alone. But with like-minded friends they abandon shame and hesitation. Just as friendship can function as a school of virtue making good people better, so can it become an incubator for evil making bad people worse. Great philosophers, however, praise philia only when it is combined with virtue and aims in a positive direction.

This deep friendship form of love, while enriching the lives of the friends, also can have profound effects upon society. Every higher religion arose among circles of friends. Geometry developed when, in ancient Greece, a band of thinkers came together to discuss circles and angles. Societies for exploration, science, and geography have been founded among friends pursuing mutual interests. Political movements, schools of art, and campaigns for and against great causes commonly spring from earnest camaraderies.

In the same way, friendship can prove subversive to society. Friends stand apart from the general mass, exclusive and private. Their associations can harbor secret and rebellious aims. People outside an assembly of friends might fear or resent it as a coterie or clique. Authorities are suspicious of such groups, which they know they can neither penetrate nor control. Dictators find them frightening.

EASE AND HARMONY

For people fallen into eros-love, philia is a graduation. Anthropologist Helen E. Fisher quotes a woman named Nisa, from the !Kung tribe of Bushmen in Africa's Kalahari Desert, describing the progression from eros to philia: "When two people are first together, their hearts are on fire and their passion is very great. After a while, the fire cools and that's how it stays. They continue to love each other, but it's in a different way—warm and dependable."

The psychologist Theodor Reik says something similar: "There is no longer the violence of [eros] love but the peacefulness of tender attachment. Indian summers of love are mellow and soft. There is a mutual identification and common experiences, joy and grief that bind two people more intimately together than romance ever did."

Philia is not as instinctive as eros. Unlike eros, it does not spring from biological origins. It does not flush our faces, tingle our tummies, or strain our nerves. It is not compulsive.

Neither is it as inquisitive as eros. Philia-lovers may speak openly if they choose, but they are not compelled to do so. Consequently they open up more readily. As eros leads to naked bodies, friendship results in exposed minds and hearts. Philia lovers confide easily, comparing views and attitudes, revealing experiences and interests, imparting plans and hopes, sharing joys and disappointments, then supporting each other in these things.

People whose ability to love is maturing within the rising scale of philia come to know and accept each other. They can relax in one another's presence. They can be themselves and feel confident of being received and appreciated as they are, rather than as they might be imagined or wished to be. They like to be with one another, enjoying going places, doing things, and resting together.

As eros loves *because*, philia loves *although*. The middle level of love cultivates a common core of tenderness, caring, understanding, passion, loyalty, trust, and ability to rise above petty annoyances. Philia helps a wife nurse her husband through an illness and a husband see his wife's frequent talking as not self-indulgence but her way of building relationship.

Deep friendship is an absolute end in itself. Philia-lovers can enjoy each other's company wholly apart from sexual considerations. They offer kindness and generous acts for the sake of the friend, with no consideration for personal pleasure, profit, or utility. As eros-love wants the other person, the higher loves also want the other person's well-being. Philia-love is rational, peaceful, stable—so extreme a contrast to eros that some people imagine they are opposites rather than a progression.

To habitual romance junkies, philia might seem unappealing. Real people and settled relationships can appear dull compared to erotic illusions and excitements. Philia dwells beyond frantic sentiment and mooning, above churning emotion and the rushing of the blood, with no surging jealousy, bitter breakups, or blissful reunions.

Philia also is freely chosen. Freedom, in fact, is one of its most sublime traits. It is a love not only free of instinct but unfettered by obligation, liberated from possessiveness, not needing to be needed, free to give or not as it chooses.

True friendship is based on equality rather than power or control. As eros-lovers often strive to dominate, higher loves seek to cultivate. Friendship does not make the absolute demands of eros-love. It is more tolerant and easygoing.

It also is more outward-looking. Eros-lovers stand face to face, gazing at each other, engrossed in one another. Philia-lovers stand side by side looking forward in the same direction. They readily work together in mutual activity: warriors battling side by side, parents raising children, philosophers shaping ideas, seekers after God praying with one another. As eros is limited to two people only, philia can include a family, a union of workers, a band of merry men. As eros is exclusive in its sentiments, philia is inclusive, welcoming kindred souls.

It also is greater in its sacrifices. As an eros-lover will die with the beloved, a philia-lover will die for the beloved. The middle love, at its best and highest, can be intensely spiritual, with the sublime sentiments and actions that we might imagine heaven to offer those who dwell there.

BUILDING PHILIA

Progress from the beginner's love of eros to the middle love of philia can happen automatically and accidentally. It can occur with no mental consciousness of the levels of love or any deliberate intention. A kind, considerate romance—as in days of old when romance was lastingly sweet—can lift romancers upward to the true, happy, deep, warm, enduring devotion of people who relish one another's company and eagerly help each other live well. Philia also can develop accidentally in many other ways.

But we shouldn't count on it. Especially in these days, when kindness, consideration, and other virtues are often remarkable for their rarity, philia is equally rare. Anyone who wants to keep love growing is wise to pursue a deliberate plan of action.

Love, like knowledge and virtue, needs to be consciously cultivated to guarantee continuance and growth from one level to the next. The promises that eros makes we must keep. As we transcend eros, the operational question no longer is "Do I love her?" but "Will I love her?" Love ceases to be a passive emotion, a mere reflex action or response to stimuli. Instead, it changes from a noun to a verb, becoming studied, considered, premeditated, voluntary, intentional, an act of the will.

Normally eros-romance cannot survive without the growth of philia to extend it further. Whatever brings lovers together, the main factor keeping them together will be friendship-love. The ancient Greeks counseled, "Emotion must warm reason, but reason must rule emotion." St. Paul's biblical letter to the Ephesians advises, ". . . husbands should love their wives as they love their own bodies." These are keys to the door from eros to philia, from thrill-love to enduring love.

The German philosopher Friedrich Nietzsche warned, "It is not lack of love but lack of friendship that makes unhappy marriages." Many modern psychologists agree, citing that couples whose marriages last have succeeded in replacing the fires of passion with the warmth of supportive companionship. As romance thrives on excitement and uncertainty, marriage thrives on stability and predictability. The old idea that romance and marriage work at cross-purposes ultimately proves logical and accurate.

"No marriage can be classified as wholly romantic or as based entirely on companionship," wrote the scholar Ernest W. Burgess in 1939. "All our data bearing on the question point to the conclusion that, on the average, marriages resulting from comradely affection turn out happier than those chiefly inspired by romantic attitudes."

Sociologists Elaine and G. William Walster observe: "Passionate love is a fragile flower; it wilts in time. Companionate love is a sturdy evergreen; it thrives with contact." They add, "Although passionate love loses its fight against time, companionate love does not."

Nancy Grote of Smith College concludes, "Society has a romantic-love complex—we view love in terms of passion and obsession." Yet, for a successful marriage, candlelight dinners, flowers, and alluring lingerie are incidental. From her study of 615 people married for an average of eighteen years, she concluded that friendship is far more important.

ABOVE PHILIA

Philia is, without a doubt, a wonderful, cozy love. Many people who achieve it stop there, pleasantly contented. Yet is this deep, intense, uplifting, and satisfying friendship-love enough? Is it sufficient to carry us through life fulfilled?

In a class on marriage, one man boasted, "Alice and I have a fifty-fifty marriage—half and half." Others in the class nodded approvingly. Giving equally and sharing loads evenly seemed a good idea, more mature than romance. Then Alice spoke up: "Yet sometimes the halves don't fit together."

And so they don't. Many people who have grown beyond eros-love and its self-serving ways carefully try to build their marriage on the fifty-fifty principle. Practicing the art of the deal, they might split their money evenly then split expenses. They might divide up cooking, take turns cleaning, alternate choice of entertainment. Yet often the sharing goes out of balance. One person is stronger willed or more conciliatory. One has a habit of assertiveness, the other defers more by nature. Where there's love, an Irish proverb goes, it is easy to halve the potato. But who wields the dividing knife? Often one of the halves comes out larger than the other.

Philia is safe, serene, and long-lasting, yet it always carries the incomplete feeling of a contract. It is a pleasant union but not union in its fullness, not everything love can be.

Some middle-lovers discover that for themselves, if they continue to grow upward on the ascending scale of love. They reach the heights of philia then move above its border to the loftiest love of all. This is the love that the ancient Greeks named *agape*.

The Highest Love

AGAPE DEFINED

IN OUR LOVE-BEFUDDLED AGE, what love *is* and is *not* is keenly debated by philosophers, theologians, and psychologists. Yet they do not argue with each other as much as with the eros-saturated, romance-infatuated, sex-inflamed society that tells us how we should live and love.

"Love is an action, an activity," asserts psychologist M. Scott Peck. "It is not a feeling."

"People generally believe that love can be reduced largely to a question of the genuineness of feeling," declares Pope John Paul II, but "love in the full sense of the word is a virtue, not just an emotion, and still less a mere excitement of the senses."

"Love is not affectionate feeling," writes popular religious thinker C. S. Lewis, "but a steady wish for the loved person's ultimate good as far as it can be obtained."

"Genuine love," elaborates psychologist Erich Fromm, ". . . is not an 'affect' in the sense of being affected by somebody, but an active striving for the growth and happiness of the loved person, rooted in one's own capacity to love."

"Love is not getting but giving," adds religious writer Henry Van Dyke, with practical simplicity.

Of course the full range of love is more varied than that if we accept the ascending scale of love. Then we comprehend love as a long progression linked to emotional-spiritual maturing: from the beginner's level of eros (or baby-love, or pleasure-love, or consumer-love); to the middle level of philia (or child-love, or fairness-love, or exchange-love); and on to the highest level of agape (or mature love, or giving-love, or producer-love). The ascending scale puts an end to the confusion over love being this or that, showing how it can take diverse forms and still be love at one level or another.

Love in its fullest definition does not leave out feelings, nor does it consist only of benevolent actions. It includes feeling and action, either or both, depending on how we manage it at any given moment. Love can get or love can give. Love can be blind or it can see acutely. Love can be evil or good. Love can destroy or exalt. Love is and does any number of things, depending on its quality, or level, on the rising scale. And that, in turn, depends on the spiritual-emotional health and maturity of the person seeking it and doing it. An awareness of love's ascending scale frees us once and for all from the perplexing riddle of what is love and what it is not.

People feel eros-love—which occupies the bottom third of the scale—in ascending degrees: from psychotic passion to hungering romance to a fond, tender, wholesome affection. People feel and do philia—the middle-love—from a guarded contractual relationship upward to a generous unity of mutually devoted companions. Yet neither of these loves is what Peck, John Paul II, Lewis, Fromm, and Van Dyke are talking about. They aim higher still, toward *agape*—the love that makes no demands on its object.

Is love possible if we want nothing from it? The very idea might alarm a me-centered eros-lover. A you-and-me-oriented philia-lover might find it nerve-wracking at the least. Yet Jesus, Confucius, the Buddha, Gandhi, Mother Teresa, and all the world's greatest lovers testify that other-centered love is not only possible but necessary for a life well-lived. Civil rights leader Martin Luther King affirmed this towering commitment, "Love is not the answer. Love is the assignment."

Agape is the classic "true love," in which the lover has no motive but the welfare of the beloved. In eros we feel, in agape we act. Eros is desire, agape a decision. Eros is a hope, agape an assurance. Eros-lovers want the other person. Agape-lovers want the other person's well-being above all things. In eros we marry the person we love. In agape we love the person we marry. Eros is a state, a condition, something passively enjoyed or endured. Agape is freely chosen and independent of any outside stimulus, motivation, or control.

Agape implies not possession but affirmation of the beloved's inherent independence and worth. Agape is not a wish to get but an effort to give, not a search for pleasure, satisfaction, or fulfillment but a persisting attempt to serve the highest good of whomever we love.

Put into action, this love becomes striving at a cost beyond any benefit we might derive, with no overriding desire to control, to receive thanks, or to reap any personal pleasure, profit, or benefit. Great philosophers of love in all ages confirm this, as do all the world's great religions.

"To love means to wish from the heart what is good for the other person, or to seek the other person's advantage," affirmed sixteenth-century religious reformer Martin Luther. Modern psychologist Rollo May writes, "We have defined agape as esteem for the other, the concern for the other's welfare beyond any gain that one can get out of it; disinterested love, typically, the love of God for man."

Is the Highest Love Selfish?

Some cynics, both ancient and modern, have denied that altruistic love can exist. They claim that even the most generous people get good feelings in return for their giving and therefore are acting in self-interest.

One influential modern explanation of altruism—the rational actor theory—defines agape as the act of a rationally self-interested person who is maximizing personal utility. Under this theory, the kindly or generous or sacrificial person behaves that way in the expectation of some return: a reward from the receiver, social praise and applause, or satisfaction with himself.

Yet this notion fails to explain why some people jeopardize their well-being and even their lives to help others. Jesus on the cross, martyrs stoned or shot, parents going hungry that their children might eat can feel wretched in the midst of their travail. "My God," Jesus cried, "why have you forsaken me?" Yet even when agape promises nothing but agony, agape-lovers do it anyway.

The doubters of agape confuse results with intentions. The highest lovers do not serve others in order to feel good, though good feelings can be a byproduct, sometimes coming as a pleasant surprise. Agape-lovers could hardly help feeling satisfied when they see their love potent, productive, and beneficial. Yet with or without happy satisfactions, agape-lovers continue to love, even when giving yields nothing but burden, loss, and pain.

Let them tell us why.

Otto Springer, the German business manager in Prague who risked everything to save Jewish people from imprisonment and death, was interviewed long after the war by Kristen Tenwick Monroe, author of *The Heart of Altruism: Perceptions of a Common Humanity*. Springer made no claim to any special credit. "One thing is important," he said. "I had no choice. I never made a moral decision to rescue Jews. I just got mad. I felt I had to do it. I came across many things that demanded my compassion."

According to Monroe, this is a common response among altruistic people. They insist that their acts of heroism or sacrifice are perfectly normal. They say they behaved only as people should under the circumstances. They also disclaim expecting any reward. They do not even feel particularly good about their conduct, seeing in it nothing extraordinary.

"Oh, let's not get too focused on me," said another of Monroe's interview subjects. "We live in one world. We are one people. Working together basically we are all the same. We can behave or we can not behave." Anyone can choose to "behave," the subject added. "We can at any moment in our lives decide to change things, and that requires courage too."

According to Monroe, altruists are distinguished by a strong consciousness of human unity. They see all people attached by common bonds of humanity, with anyone and everyone deserving concern.

It is this sense of human connection that leads them to see their heroism as nothing special. To them their acts seem only common sense, common concern, common caring, simply how a person of integrity and dignity should live. For these people, caring—in feeling, perhaps, but even more in action—becomes a primary moral impetus. As the twelfth-century French religious thinker St. Bernard of Clairvaux observed, agape-love "seeks no cause beyond itself and no limit; it is its own fruit, its own enjoyment. I love because I love; I love in order that I may love."

Agape in Action

The first task of the highest love is to resist the urgings of self. Emotional maturity begins only when we seek to give to others attentive understanding and assistance without expecting personal returns.

The conquest of egotism is the highest achievement any human being can aspire to. The nineteenth-century French philosopher and sociologist Auguste Comte and, after him, the English philosopher Herbert Spencer named this great activity "altruism" from the Italian word *altrui*, or others.

"Not until he attains to altruism is man in a condition to maintain himself in society and in nature," wrote the nineteenth-century German-Hungarian psychologist Max Nordau. He pointed out that as long as a person is engrossed in self he can have no clear vision of the world beyond himself and, therefore, cannot deal with it effectively.

In *The Weight of Glory*, C. S. Lewis points out that many people, if asked to name the highest virtue, would answer "unselfishness." Yet that misses the point, or at best meets it only half way. The "un" of unselfishness marks it as negative. It suggests not so much gaining good for others as doing without it ourselves, as though our abstinence, rather than their enrichment, were the goal. This interpretation of love as unselfishness can be a trick of the ego, focusing upon self and thus distorting altruism.

Actually, the self should never be neglected, scorned, denigrated, or martyred without good cause. Altruistic love at its loftiest means service to the cause of life. That includes promoting one's own greatest good along with that of other people, seeking a reasonable apportionment of life-giving endeavors.

All higher love is rooted in what Erich Fromm calls a productive way of living—as opposed to the "I want, I need, gimmie-gimmie" consumer orientation of modern eros and present-day society in general. Agape-love has no room for calculated self-pleasing, neither for careful contractual stipulations of so much and no more. Such considerations are irrelevant to the real unity of "we," in which each person, like an organ in a body, is part of a whole rather than a solitary individual bumping up against others.

Fromm explains: "Genuine [agape] love is an expression of productiveness and implies care, respect, responsibility, and knowledge." All these traits are essential to its practice and growth. Let us examine them in reverse order for possible greater clarity.

✦ We cannot love who we do not know, as any number of great saints and lovers have said. We have to comprehend what a person needs before we can begin to serve her or his well-being. This requires both transparency from the beloved and insight in the lover.

✦ A sense of responsibility for the beloved is the first motivation for effort. Acting upon it is likely to uncover reasons for still more responsibility.

✦ Respect for the person allows no looking down from on high, no sense of a superior donating to an inferior. The importance of the beloved is fully equal to the lover's, seated in the soul where all people hold equal worth. This bedrock awareness of human value inspires and sustains the depth of respect that agape needs to function fully.

✦ The central virtue of all love is care. Care also is the source of love— every kind of love, from eros to agape. For love to exist at all, the lover first must care—the opposite of indifference, which in no way could lead to either the excitement of eros or the difficult choices of agape. With eros, especially at its lower levels, care is largely about the self— what I can get for my real or imagined fulfillment. With agape, care looks toward others and devotes its efforts to their fulfillment. Around care are ordered many subsidiary virtues: honesty, self-control, faithfulness, fairness, wisdom, courage, gratitude, perseverance, humility, hope.

With agape-love, there is none of the passivity of passion, nothing automatic, few sweet accidents. Intentional insight, effort, and action are constantly demanded for this loftiest love. When we care for the beloved in this way, we want that person to gain as much or more than we do, and this shall make us happy. At times we live more for the beloved than for ourselves. In doing so, we never consider ourselves martyred, nor do we feel deserving of praise. Sacrifice is our gift and giving our privilege. Yet, perhaps as a divine irony, the more we give with generous motives, the more sublimely joy flows through our lives.

Unlike eros, agape never is blind. Rather, this love observes keenly, perceives deeply, and is sightless only to despair and hopelessness. With life-giving vision, the highest love discerns human potential and helps it come into being. The highest love strives with the opportunities at hand to create conditions for people to develop their highest capacities. This nurturing love can be given equally to wife or husband, to a child or a classroom of children, to employees or employer, to governed or governors, to an institution or a cause.

Since agape-love is a choice, it remains wholly within our charge. It is a love we can guarantee: reliable, growing, and lasting. Unlike eros, where emotions control us and come and go capriciously, agape-love finds its limits only in the capacities and abilities of the lover. And these increase with exercise. The more love of this kind we produce, the more we become capable of producing it.

When we give the highest love, we work toward our own abdication. Our goal is to make ourselves superfluous, placing the beloved in a condition of prosperity where our gifts no longer are needed. We nurture our children so that someday they can nurture themselves. We teach our students so they will come to know what we know and more. We help to build a whole person so the person will be complete without us, independent of us, perhaps superior to us. Being no longer needed is our sign of success and therefore one of our great rewards.

Whom Should We Love?

Agape sees every living person as a being of value and wishes everyone well. As American philosopher Lewis Mumford observed, "Love is concerned, fundamentally, with the nurture of life at every occasion; it is the practice of bestowing life on other creatures and receiving life from them." When we love in this way we strive, to one extent or another, to love everyone we encounter. An agape-lover's whole relationship to life is love.

As the highest love flows from the lover in all directions, its appropriate expressions differ. We love husbands and wives differently in degree and action from strangers. We love our children, our employers, and beggars on the street in different ways. Yet all people, even all life on earth, can come under the umbrella of agape-love's potential care and responsibility.

This idea of universal love possibly originated with the ancient Greek philosophy of Stoicism. Adherents to this school of thought, which acknowledged the all-pervasive presence of a universal force, or God, saw all people to be part of a unified world in which everyone's well-being is linked and interdependent. Stoics felt obliged to live as *kosmopolitai*, or world-citizens, respecting the humanity in every person everywhere equally. The philosophy also required that all people be accepted as ends in themselves, rather than as means to other ends.

Stoicism's world citizenship required benevolence toward the poor and the sick, hospitality toward foreigners, and strict limits on harshness in war. No one should be despised or disadvantaged because of race, ethnicity, nationality, gender, or other accidents of birth. The Stoics became the first thinkers in Western tradition to urge equal citizenship and education for women.

Jewish scriptural doctrine upholds similar principles, requiring humane treatment for widows and orphans, debtors and the poor, strangers and aliens. Christian teaching goes on to regard all people everywhere, including enemies, as God's creations to be generously loved.

While eros favors people who seem easy to love, agape also strives to love the unlovable. If we direct our love only toward people we find agreeable, or who share our point of view, or who will be grateful, or who we deem to deserve our pity, then the highest love has not yet blossomed in us fully. This truest of true loves is patient and long-suffering, graciously bearing with people who are difficult, aggravating, or demanding. Agape at its best is indomitable in expressing good will and indifferent to discouragement.

It is capable of loving the dim-witted, the ill, the malformed, the morose, the sneering, the criminal, the enemy. Just as it is not inflamed by attractiveness, it is not quenched by unattractiveness. As Martin Luther explained, this true love says, "I love you not because you are good or bad; for I draw my love not from your goodness, as from another's fountain, but from my own little spring, from the word which is grafted in my heart and which bids me to love my neighbor."

As difficult as this might be at times, the lover's need for forbearance and effort lessens with practice. Not only does the agape-lover grow bigger-hearted with the exercise of love. He also, when he pours himself out in aid of anyone or anything, finds affectionate feelings arising for the object of his efforts. These feelings, as well as growing skills and power in love, ease his burdens.

Religious thinkers compare human agape to God's love for sinners, who are loved not because they are worthy but only because God is love, and to love is God's nature. While agape is not motivated by any value in the beloved, it inevitably creates value in whoever receives it.

Agape's Limits

From the outside looking in, agape-love seems austere, difficult, dangerous, and all but impossible to sustain. It appears more idealistic than realistic, at best only an occasional pursuit.

Doesn't the highest love leave the lover dangerously vulnerable? Isn't it foolish, even suicidal, a willing journey into the cannibal kingdom to be eaten alive? By purely rational standards such objections seem well founded. Psychoanalyst Erich Fromm, though a strong spokesman for agape, points out that great saints, have, on average, short life spans.

Agape is utterly impractical, even impossible for you or me to attain for more than furtive moments by our own intentions and power. But here religions' thinkers enter the picture. Human beings, they say, as children of God, are empowered to achieve agape directly by God's grace and love. It is inconceivable that anyone could love this way for long without divine intervention. We need power beyond our own immediate potency for the discernment, strength, and courage that agape demands. And, whether or not we embrace any particular theology, we receive such power when we seek to give love in this most humanly effective manner.

Yet the agape-lover will encounter hardships, even failures. For a variety of reasons the highest love can falter. It can fall short of perfection because of our own insufficient ability to love. We might mistakenly give the kind of gifts that we ourselves would like to have, without enough regard for how well they suit the receiver. Our serving might attempt to construct the kind of life we feel a loved one should live, with too little attention to the wishes and needs of the beloved.

Even when our insight and ability are sound, we cannot be sure that our love will prove effective. Everybody needs the highest love, but not everybody wants it. Some egotistical people can accept love only as a kind of tribute. They long to be idolized, as eros creates idols. They want to be loved for their attributes, real or imagined: for their beauty, charm, or cleverness, their good taste, their usefulness. If we serve such people only because we love, they can experience our service as an offense. Put in the position of beneficiaries, they are left feeling poor, needy, humiliated.

Selfish people might dislike agape-love for other reasons as well. Often it is unsentimental. It can express itself firmly, even toughly. In its concern for human welfare, it might fail to please anyone concerned too little for his own genuine well-being.

Worse still, from the standpoint of the selfish, this love is not under their control. A man cannot manipulate it with honeyed words. A woman cannot exploit it with a wiggle of her hips. Agape refuses to indulge every wish, whim, and impulse. It resists pressures and appeals, not serving demands but answering perceived needs by way of inner promptings.

If a receiver is untruthful, this noble, serving love can be deflected, wasted, lavished on an image of a person who does not really exist. People who are hostile, aggressive, or defensive can render agape impotent if it proves insufficient to neutralize their resistance.

For the giver, a failed effort to love can feel disappointing, wearying, and costly. Yet agape nonetheless remains the least risky of all the forms of love. It is never lost entirely, never wholly wasted. Derived from infinite resources beyond ourselves, this sacrificial giving springs from wealth and plenty and has no limits. It can be offered freely with no fear of being squandered or futile. If it for some reason is not well used, it flows back to soften and expand the heart of the lover. Meanwhile, it inspires other people who observe it.

So agape, unlike eros, never dies. It lives richly and memorably in the hearts of the beloved and the lover then ripples outward far beyond both. Often its results blossom forth in wholly unexpected ways, touching and inspiring people far and wide, moving down through future generations, animating nations, enriching civilizations. Thus does agape-love become the pinnacle and fulfillment of total love.

Growing up to Agape

While giving, serving love can be taught and recommended, it never should be pressed upon people as a duty. By comparison with agape, duty is dry, brittle, lacking in eager willingness. Duty's motive force comes from the outside, not from within the lover. Duty serves only as a plaster cast around broken love to keep it functioning. It can even lead to mimicry, an outward pose or posture that yields no inward emotional benefits.

Growing up to be an agape-lover is not accomplished in one great leap. Rather, it is a continuing process, often rigorous and usually slow. In our sensuous and selfish social setting, merely rising above the sicklier forms of eros is an awkward and confusing task. Ascending into philia is difficult and noble in itself. If we are rising on the scale of love, we will come into agape only little by little.

Invitations to overlay the lower loves with the highest love are never absent. They are offered by opportunities for compassion. They are extended as choices to be patient, kind, and generous under frustration, friction, and irritation.

If only she were less talkative, more sexy, less extravagant, more attentive, he might be tempted to think, then I'd love her better. If only he was more considerate, a better listener, more sensitive, and earned more money, she might ruminate, then I could love him more easily. If only they weren't so noisy, demanding, infuriating, and would pick up their toys, I could love them perfectly.

All the daily trials that call for tolerance, forbearance, and forgiveness are calls for us to abandon the "if" and practice the highest love regardless. A great sign of love between spouses is acceptance. The surest sign of love for children is patience.

Only when we willingly and graciously submit day by day and year upon year to the endless inconveniences and sacrifices of love can the truest love continue, as once we promised, eternally.

Agape and Christianity

Agape is by no means exclusive to the religion founded by Jesus Christ. As the noted philanthropist and philosopher Sir John Templeton points out in his book *Agape Love: A Tradition Found in Eight World Religions*, the theme of love as selfless service is a major principle of religious faiths worldwide.

Buddhists offer a path of compassion in which caring for others becomes the motivating force of life. Confucianism and Taoism regard transcendent love as a vital part of true wisdom. Hindus set forth a branch of yoga known as the heart-centered path that leads to enlightenment by love for deity in the form of loving all humanity. Equally do Judaism and Islam advocate altruistic love. Thus do the varied teachings of the highest love reflect the unity of all humanity.

Followers of Christ were first to use "agape" as a noun describing the ideal of active, benevolent love. In Christian tradition, agape is known as the first fruit of the Holy Spirit, the preeminent grace, God's love flowing through one person to bless another. As Scandinavian Bishop

Anders Nygren put it, "All love that has any right to be called Agape is nothing else but an outflow from the Divine Love. It has its source in God. 'God is Agape.'"

With God's divine nature as an all-sufficient being, he reigns over his creation with this supreme level of love. Any lesser form of love would be absurd in the context of the faith. For example, how might we express the often-quoted statement of his love from the Gospel of John in terms of eros, philia, and agape?

+ Eros: God so loved the world that he enjoyed pleasurable feelings about it, wanted it, needed it, and couldn't live without it. That makes no sense at all.
+ Philia: God so loved the world that he agreed to a fair deal, giving it what it gave him. That's no better. But . . .
+ Agape: "God so loved the world that he gave his only begotten Son, that whoever believes in him should not perish but have everlasting life." That passage (John 3:16), a favorite among evangelists, suggests the one kind of love that God bestows upon his creation. God's love must be all-giving agape, always.

Christians, in order to be true followers of Christ, are exhorted to aspire to the same giving, serving, sacrificial love in every aspect of their lives. The first and greatest commandments of the faith are to love God with all one's being, and then to love one's neighbor as oneself.

In *The Life of the Beloved* theologian Henri J. M. Nouwen writes about people's love for God in return: "The unfathomable mystery of God is that God is a Lover who wants to be loved. The one who created us is waiting for our response to the love that gave us our being. God not only says: 'You are my Beloved.' God also asks: 'Do you love me?' and offers us countless chances to say yes."

But what, on earth, does loving God mean? In the 1769 Authorized King James translation of the Bible, agape was called "charity," but in later translations it was rendered, simply, as "love." Given our society's confusion about the meaning of love, it might be easy to imagine that loving God amounts to feeling fond of God for giving us so many nice things, or perhaps working up something of a crush on our Divine benefactor.

Yet the Bible says nothing of the sort. Whenever the Scriptures mention loving God, they link it with obedience to his will. Loving God is seeking and doing his will—nothing more and never anything less. Jesus' dearest friend, the Apostle John, says in the New Testament, "The love of God consists in this: that we keep his commandments" (1 John 5:3).

As earthly things must be known to be loved, God must be loved to be known. Only by obeying God can we come to comprehend him in any sense at all. Meanwhile, the three levels of love cannot endure much burden nor yield much benefit without God's grace. For their sake, as well as ours, we must give all loves second place to God's will and commands.

Loving our neighbor offers one of the best and most frequent opportunities to obey the greatest commandment. This means striving toward the highest love in romance, friendship, and wedlock, in raising children, conducting business, and meeting people in the street. The lesser levels of love can come or go without urgent spiritual consequence, but agape-love is the necessary act of every Christian.

As this love is the soul of a godly life, so must it be the heart of every virtue. Without it, faith is ideology; hope is self-centeredness; forgiveness is self-demeaning; fortitude is imprudence; justice is legalism; generosity is extravagance; perseverance is stubbornness; care is obligation; fidelity is servility. Every virtue is confirmed by the love that accompanies it. The sixteenth-century Spanish mystic St. Teresa of Avila stated, "Our Lord does not care so much for the importance of our works as for the love with which they are done."

"A new commandment I give you: love one another," says Jesus. But not as the world loves, he cautions. "As I have loved," he adds, "so you must love one another" (John 13:34–35). Not long after saying that, he lay down his life for his friends and for all of lost humanity.

Love, as referred to in the New Testament, is always genuine concern and active care that helps people grow toward wholeness and fulfillment and attain their eternal destiny in God's kingdom. Again as the Apostle

Paul describes: "Love is patient and kind; love is not jealous or boast-ful; it is not arrogant or rude. Love does not insist on its own way; it is not irritable or resentful; it does not rejoice at wrong, but rejoices in the right. Love bears all things, believes all things, hopes all things, endures all things" (1 Corinthians 13:4–7).

St. Paul affirmed that all human contact, including sexual relations, should be directed by the spiritual force of agape. To better distinguish selfish eroticism from the apostle's ideal of sexual agape, we can use the exquisite definition of agape offered by the eighteenth-century German philosopher Baron Gottfried Wilhelm von Leibniz: "joy through another's bliss." This integrates sexual love with agape, profane love with the sacred, by stressing the self-giving of the highest love, which is absent from the sensate notion of love as desire. Curiously, in line with this logic, the fifth-century theologian St. Augustine affirmed that sex-ual desire initially was created as a free choice, becoming involuntary only after the fall of Adam and Eve in the Garden of Eden.

Without the highest level of love, Christianity is hollow and false. The Apostle Paul attests to this: "If I speak in the tongues of men and of angels, but have not love, I am a noisy gong or a clanging cymbal. And if I have prophetic powers, and understand all mysteries and all knowledge, and if I have all faith, so as to remove mountains, but have not love, I am nothing. If I give away all I have, and if I deliver my body to be burned, but have not love, I gain nothing" (1 Corinthians 13: 1–3). The Apostle John goes further, saying: "Whoever does not love abides in death" (1 John 3:14).

Of course, godly people are not expected to practice perfect love from the beginning. Like anyone else, they can only aspire and strive toward agape. Frequently they will fall short of the highest love as they progress in their personal spiritual growth. St. Bernard of Clairvaux expressed this in his work *De diligendo Dei*. He described the proper course of love to be one of ascent from self-love, which is humanity's natural con-dition, to pure love for God.

St. Bernard also believed that love has stages, steps, or levels—four of them, in his theological schema. All human love begins as self-love, simply because of how we are made. "Since human nature is frail and weak, man finds himself compelled by force of circumstance to serve himself first. This is the carnal love by which man loves himself for his own sake." This self-love is wholly normal and acceptable. Yet if it is allowed to go on without limit, it threatens to run out of control and turn destructive.

The commandment to love our neighbors as ourselves puts the necessary limit on self-serving and turns the course of our love upward toward the next progressive level. "Thus the natural love becomes social when it is extended into what is common," wrote St. Bernard. Carnal love then is broadened and begins to lose some of its strictly egocentric character.

Yet if love for neighbor is to grow perfect, it must find its ground in God and in our love for him. God awakens within us love of him by sending us hardships then delivering us from them. Discovering our own helplessness, we learn what we possess in God. Once carnally minded and loving no one but ourselves, we begin to love God for the use we can make of him. God remains within the sphere of our self-love, but loving God even in this limited way creates new possibilities.

When God continues to lavish kindness upon us, our love toward him is broadened and deepened. Our heart is softened by his beneficence and goodness. In time, we no longer love him mainly for what we can get from him but for his own sake.

In the final and loftiest stage of love, our soul becomes, as it were, drunk with divine love. It forgets itself entirely and loves itself only in God. This state belongs to heavenly existence. Under earthly conditions great saints experience it only in rare and solitary moments. So said St. Bernard of Clairvaux of the Christian's levels of love.

Meanwhile the Old Testament's Psalm 89 has God saying that "love is built to last forever." The New Testament agrees: The Apostle Paul writes, "Love never ends; as for prophecies, they will pass away; as for tongues, they will cease; as for knowledge, it will pass away. For our knowledge is imperfect and our prophecy is imperfect; but when the perfect comes, the imperfect will pass away. . . . So faith, hope, love abide, these three; but the greatest of these is love" (1 Corinthians 13:8–13).

Overcoming Love's Enemies

"BUT I DON'T WANT TO GO AMONG MAD PEOPLE,"
ALICE REMARKED.
"OH, YOU CAN'T HELP THAT," SAID THE CAT,
"WE ARE ALL MAD HERE."
—*LEWIS CARROLL (1832–1898)*

LOVE HAS MANY ENEMIES. Its immediate foes include jealousy, suspicion, and possessiveness; secretiveness and betrayal of confidence; greed, envy, and stinginess; resentment and vindictiveness; rudeness, arrogance, stubbornness, and neglect; habits of criticism and disparagement; perfectionism, manipulation, competitiveness, and insisting on one's own way. That is quite a list in itself, and it is not complete.

Dishonesty ranks among the worst of love's enemies. That can confuse, even ruin everything. Defensive lies, malicious lies, white lies, social lies, face-saving lies, and all the other kinds of lies that people tell and excuse themselves for telling can block relationship by deflecting love, preventing love from developing, or poisoning love.

According to one sociological study, the average American tells 200 lies per day. Be that as it may, much of the confusion, pain, and personal tragedy of failed love can be avoided if people determine to be honest and open with each other from the start. If they feel that truth is too harsh, then they need to develop more tact, discretion, kindness, and a good sense of timing. If they feel they can't afford truth at all, then they have some personal character cleansing to do before they're ready for beneficial loving relationships.

All of the immediate enemies of love are obvious and can be dealt with one by one as they arise. Yet other adversaries of love lurk at the very heart of the culture that surrounds us, infiltrates us, and operates within our being. As sickly as the culture itself, these enemies of love run deeper and are more difficult to recognize. They require acutely conscious living to combat and overcome.

One profound enemy of love in our time is the institutionalization of self-centeredness. Though the voice of the society comes across confusing and contradictory, in general it teaches something like this: Take as much as you can get and yield less in return. Too many among us are seduced by this corrosive leading.

A second, root problem obstructing love is the failure of people who follow the culture to mature in their emotional being. These two basic enemies of love are related in a circular way. Self-centeredness impedes emotional maturing, which in turn perpetuates self-centeredness.

Eat Your Neighbor

Consumers consume consumer goods, and when those are not enough they consume each other. That's a rule in a dog-eat-dog society, the principle behind look out for number one, up yours, and get your retaliation first. We see it operating in marketplace and office, in romance and marriage, in child abuse, thievery, and thrill-killing.

Emotionally stunted and unproductive people are a fact of modern life. They live like walking appetites, consuming, squandering, destroying to satisfy bloated or perverse needs. Such excessive consuming can end only in war, the ultimate blood-price of empty, super-hungry, undeveloped people venting frustration and hate on one another.

Not that consuming is harmful or evil in itself. Limited consuming is perfectly justified to meet the needs of healthy survival. It is a necessity of nature, how we're made. We all must eat, clothe ourselves, and gain shelter from the elements to stay alive and thriving. Beyond raw survival, all moral standards also allow for reasonable pleasures and comforts. Nothing is wrong with such basic consuming, which in fact is very much right, as a Jewish tradition of "consecrated consumption" affirms.

Where the modern world goes wrong is not in consuming to live, but in living to consume. Consumerism is carried to the fevered extremes of an all-consuming obsession. Not long ago people felt proud to be producers, workers, contributors, providers. Now the society lumps us all into the category of "consumers," as if we were little more than ever-gobbling mouths and manure machines. Plato's "Commonwealth of Swine" rules not only in the West but is spreading around the world as people everywhere fall under its seductive influence.

Consumerism leads people to experience the world mainly through the eyes of desire. Not merely a habit, it grows into a mentality, an emotional fixation, a spiritual dysfunction, a vast mass delusion. Materialism, like power and eros-love, becomes a desperate way to complete an unfulfilled and emotionally underdeveloped self, a method of absorbing something from the outside to appease inner emptiness.

Consumerism shapes attitudes, twists behavior, grinds down ethical feeling. Its ethos cancels out such virtues as contentment, generosity, self-denial, and patience, while cultivating self-oriented, ravenous, devouring distortions of character. Where once people strove for grand achievements, now they aspire to win the lottery and live out their days like oversized infants on the productivity of others.

Residing in a society that rewards few virtues but monetary success, people who once were bonded to each other in humane and respectful communities are reduced to inhuman abstractions. They become anonymous consumers whose ties to each other are based upon ability to pay. This is witnessed best by the very poor among us: no cash, no connection, no personhood.

The social order, dedicated to private and not public enterprise, pits each person against the others, individual success against the common good. Life threatens to become a merciless contest with hardly more meaning than the zoological ups and downs of beast-life in a jungle. People as chronic competitors live apart by habit and nature, abysmally alone. Ultimately, every man for himself implies an emergency situation—or creates one.

Does consumerism engender empty, wanting people, or do everhungry people generate consumerism? Actually, the relationship between the two is cyclical. A general diminishment of humane caring brings on an emotional vacuum. Commerce eagerly leaps forward to fill it. This allows people to stuff their emptiness with merchandise and disconnect themselves all the more from their fellows.

Salesmen might imagine that the consumer mentality stops with vending and acquiring commodities. But that is only the beginning. Consumerism becomes a relationship with the world. It stares hungrily at the whole environment. Mad waste of natural resources is counted a measure of productivity even while it wreaks heedless ecological damage and destruction. Other people, also part of the environment, equally are seen instrumentally as things to be used and devoured. The triumph of consumption turns the whole society into a vast human food chain, a community of predators and victims.

As cited in an earlier chapter, psychologist Erich Fromm observes that in any social order love relationships are only a more intense expression of the general human relatedness that prevails in the culture. Thus in the consumer society we foster consumer-love. Man seeks to feed on woman sexually: "a dish," "scrumptious," "delicious." Woman uses her "hunk" to fix her car, kill a mouse, take out the garbage, give her sex, buy her a diamond.

Wedlock, at its best a lifelong commitment made in a spirit of service to foster offspring, instead becomes just another consumer tactic to meet personal needs and desires. Our language reveals that: Rather than "marrying," we "*get* married," just as we get anything else. Since needs and wants change with time, along with people's ability to meet them, monogamy logically gives way to a succession of partners. Meanwhile, children become an inconvenience: They cost a lot of money, limit personal choices, create burdens. While economists coolly calculate the cost of maintaining a child from diaper days through university years, we are led to reconsider the continuance of life.

Sickened consumerism also turns covetous eyes on the kiddies. As a healthy culture nurtures its young, a culture shifted into pathological reverse feeds on its young. Even when children are safe from abuse at home, they face dangers everywhere else from predator-consumers who would poison their Halloween candy, strip off their clothes, or snuff out their lives.

With consumers in great numbers regressing rather than growing in spiritual-emotional health, all of society can only turn about and function backwards. In such a social order, leaders no longer inspire but dominate, living on the energy of their followers. Followers, feeling misused and betrayed, disparage the leaders or murmur of rebellion. Employers feed on employees who in turn, withdraw loyalty and dedication. When people strive for the "good life" of appetite, their lives can leave only trails of debris. In time the whole social order threatens to disintegrate into anarchy.

Working as a journalist in the shattered state of Yugoslavia during its civil war of the 1990s, I heard of a military commander who went from village to village slaughtering people randomly under the policy of "ethnic cleansing." An old friend asked him, "How could you do this when you were taught to love your neighbor?" The officer replied, "I do love my neighbors. I love killing them."

Failing to Grow

What manner of person fails to love effectively? The social conformist, we might say, if we blame the society for our inadequate love—and to a large extent we are right in doing that. Psychologist Erich Fromm observed that present-day society is so thoroughly founded on egotism that it leaves people virtually incapable of effective loving. Certainly a social order that trains its members to profound self-centeredness must accept much responsibility for their condition.

Yet the person who conforms to the leading of such a society hardly can be held faultless. We all are responsible to some degree for whatever we conform to. The outside voice of the society has found a personal inward response. When the voice leads us away from the needs of life—and effective love certainly is one of those needs—something within the person who assents also is amiss.

We might think of the conformist to selfish social norms as emotionally immature, retarded, underdeveloped, stunted, atrophied, degenerate. This spiritual-emotional deficiency is, of course, the illness that renders the "sick society" unwell, a personal ailment magnified to a major social epidemic and cultural disaster.

Yet what is the nature of the sickness itself? Consumerism? Materialism? A failure to love effectively? All these might be cited as possible diagnoses. Yet they seem as much results as causes, more like symptoms of a broader malfunction.

May I suggest that the problem, at its root, is a failure to grow sufficiently? This failure we see overwhelming the society is, in fact, a kind of retrogression practiced by vast and increasing numbers of people. They individually, and the society collectively, are not growing toward healthy human wholeness. Nor are they resting at some neutral state, waiting there, marking time. Rather, they are sliding with accelerating speed into sickness of emotions, mind, and body. (Please note that order: emotions, mind, and body; the deterioration proceeds in exactly that sequence.)

They are not advancing toward higher maturity, nor holding ground at some stable point, but regressing ever faster into immaturity. Instead of struggling toward wholesomeness, they are willingly, eagerly embracing unwholesomeness.

So this human deterioration is not just absence of growth, nor some starting point before growth begins. It is, instead, a striving backward, a strong drive downward toward decay and ultimate destruction. It is anti-growth, a sometimes unconscious but powerful death wish, an active momentum against the force of life.

When people fail to grow physically, mentally, or emotionally, what are the consequences? Clearly such people do not remain like infants—sweet, charming, and cute. They grow anyway. But their growth is not healthy. It is stunted, twisted, deformed.

We see this clearly where physical growth somehow has failed. Then people have developed as midgets or dwarfs. Seriously failed mental growth produces ignoramuses or, in cases of congenital retardation, conditions that psychologists once described with terms like moron, imbecile, and idiot. And how should we describe failure of emotional growth? Similar terms will do. A person whose emotional faculty has fallen short of healthy development can be thought of as suffering emotional dwarfism or spiritual retardation.

In every kind of failed growth, some degree of human malfunction is the consequence. The person does not do nearly as well in life as if things had turned out right. This is obvious in the case of stunted bodies, which cannot move about and accomplish adult-sized tasks as readily as if they had grown properly. It is equally clear regarding retardation of the mind; its victims face serious mental limitations in their lives. People suffering emotional retardation probably suffer worst from their condition, because their lack is both more limiting and more painful. They endure a condition of stunted sensitivity, deformed feelings, and endless, insatiable want.

To understand more fully the nature of this anti-growth and its damaging effects upon people, we must reason out first why people should grow, then how they should go about it. I say "reason out" because we are compelled to rediscover such things for ourselves. We are beginning afresh—from nothing, as it were. Healthy human growth and its desirability are generally forgotten in our faltering society. They are lost to "experts" and laymen alike, buried out of sight beneath eruptions of decay that pile ever thicker over present-day culture like lava over ancient Pompeii.

Yet like all basic facts of human existence, the reason for growth and how we can achieve it are relatively easy matters to understand. We don't need experts to see such things for us. We can see them for ourselves with the vision of our own common sense.

Raising the Inner Child

First, why should people grow at all? It is reasonable to say, as Aristotle suggested, that *growth is the purpose of life*. This is a statement at once profound and simple. It is profound in stating why we are on earth, in probing the reason for human existence. It is simple in recommending what we must do in order to lead lives of genuine fulfillment.

As long as each of us is alive, we should be a work in progress. We always should be under construction: building a strength, a skill, an area of learning, a trait of character. We always should be moving toward an open-ended goal of improvement, pressing on, becoming more and better. We should exist not so much as human beings but as human becomings.

Of course, life's purpose can be expressed in other terms besides growing: to glorify God, to save the soul, to attain Nirvana, to actualize or individualize the self. But in all these expressions, growing still remains both the central purpose of our existence and our method of achieving it.

That growth is the purpose of life, in biological terms, is self-evident. Growth, life—they are virtually identical. Growing is all that life really does, life in any of its forms. Grass and giraffes, leopards and lichens, petunias and people—they all grow as long as they are living healthily, and when they stop growing they begin to die.

We as human beings start fulfilling this purpose of life as babies. At that stage, growing happens pretty automatically. The main way a baby grows is physically. To do this, the infant needs proper feeding and exercise—all very simple.

As the child gets older, the main emphasis of growth shifts to the intellectual, which is less automatic. Though body-growth is still important, the child works mainly to develop his or her mind, learning language, mathematics, and all the other things the intellect must know to bring a person through life in the surrounding society. Again, the method of growing is first by feeding and then by exercise.

Our culture feeds up our bodies well and gives us ample means to exercise to gain strength. It also trains our intellects enormously, more than any other culture in history. But there our culture largely stops leading us upward. Our society largely overlooks growth as an enduring purpose of our existence. It suggests that people have grown quite enough by a particular time that the society regards to be an age of maturity.

People are finished and complete perhaps by their eighteenth year, when they can buy cigarettes and vote; or by twenty-one, when they can get hard liquor; or maybe by thirty if they go on for a doctorate degree. Their bodies are developed, their intellects, too, and after that they're at cruising altitude.

It is hard to imagine a belief more tragic. If people stop growing at that point, they are threatened with their lives becoming a waste. They've missed something vitally important. They've fallen way short. They've neglected the most important of all aspects of human development.

Beyond physical growth and intellectual growth lies a third kind of growing. Some time in adulthood, the emphasis of our growing should shift again. Our bodily growth is just about ended. Our intellectual growth has come along well, though it can and should continue all through our lives. But more vital to a successful life than any other kind of growing is what might be called emotional-spiritual development.

That's a straggly term—emotional-spiritual—or, if you like, spiritual-emotional. Yet it's appropriate because the emotional and spiritual merge and blend like intertwining fingers. Where one leaves off and the other begins is impossible to say. Perhaps we can call the third kind of growth, for the sake of simplicity, growing in the emotional part of our being.

The emotional part is not only feelings but a whole faculty, as important as our body and our mind, even more so. These three basic faculties do different things for us. Our physical faculty produces mobility. Our intellectual faculty produces ideas, calculations, memory, forecasts. Likewise, our emotional faculty produces feelings, inspirations, insight, will, discernment, wisdom, intuition, courage, and probably a good many other things useful for worthwhile living. Imagine life without healthy feelings, inspirations, insight, intuition, and wisdom, and you'll gain a good idea of how important this part of us is.

Yet before our emotional faculty can do its job well, it, too, like body and intellect, must grow. Exactly as we must grow physically and mentally from infancy to mature adulthood, so should the important emotional-spiritual side of us be growing, from self-centered, self-absorbed, self-pleasing infantilism to a mature, balanced, active interest and concern about things beyond the self.

It's really very simple and obvious: People must mature emotionally or they remain mere fragments. As we already have observed, if one or another of these three facets of development is seriously lacking, a person is incomplete and lame, or crippled, or disadvantaged, or developmentally disabled—unable to function in an optimal way.

Equally obvious is the manner by which this spiritual-emotional part of us is supposed to grow. For healthy emotional development, any baby, and any child, and any adult should be fed in a healthy way and then encouraged to exercise.

And how are we fed emotionally? The principle emotional feeding is altruistic love—active care, respect, responsibility, and knowledge directed toward the welfare and growth of the person loved.

Just as exercise is fully as important as feeding for bodily development and intellectual growth, so is emotional exercise needed, in addition to feeding, for growth. And how do we achieve that? We give altruistic love to everyone around us, as much as we possibly can.

The result of proper feeding and exercise in all of our major faculties is rounded, holistic, total growth and thoroughly healthy, wholesome people. Our bodies, well cared for, are strong and robust, feel well, look well, and are well. Our minds are informed and able to think accurately and reason clearly. Emotionally, too, we are sound and fit: independently happy and content, not ruled by impulse or circumstance, guided from within, humanly productive, able to judge wisely and choose well the things that benefit life and lead us in a lifetime of healthy growing. When we choose to grow in all three of our faculties—physical, intellectual, and emotional-spiritual—we are guaranteed the fullest, most abundant, and satisfying life.

We can make a plan for spiritual-emotional growth—as we make plans for bodily and mental growth. The world's great religions all offer such a plan, though often it is obscured by a crust of theology. There is no age limit for this aspect of growth, nor any point of completion, nor an age of decline. Growing in the spiritual-emotional side of our being can and should go on and on, however long we may live.

Looking at our own past, we might object that we never received enough effective love to move ahead in healthy emotional growing. Until we get adequate "feeding," how can we exercise—how can we have much to give?

The only solution is to look for love. But we probably have done that already without success. Many people, acknowledging the absence of love in their lives, yearn for love, hunger for it, search, beg, pine, seduce, and demand. Young people, old people, and those in between try to get love from one another. Yet that effort is not working, since few people have enough to give. Where, then, do we get the love we need?

The world's great religions answer that question, too, and we need not be formally religious to put their answer to work. Abundant love is always available for anyone. When the human fund runs low, we can get all we need from God, a higher power, or whatever we care to call the cosmic source of life. To nonreligious people, that might sound mysterious, and it is. But never mind. God is love, God has love, and God will give love to us in abundance. We have only to do the will of a benign God, which is to live in accord with truth, right, and love. Then from the source of all love we will be endlessly revitalized.

Why Love?

15

TO LOVE OR NOT TO LOVE

NEITHER LIFELONG GROWTH nor total love is easy. They might be simple to understand, but they always remain hard to master. They are greatly time-consuming, uncomfortable at moments, costly in effort, and deeply humbling. They hold no promise of fame, wealth, or social status, though the emotional rewards for ourselves and people around us prove far greater than any of life's outward gains.

Persisting with healthy growth and love constitutes never-ending tasks. For those of us who embrace the course of personal growing and complete loving, once the decision is made it becomes a lifetime commitment. No matter how long we live, we will never be finished, never be able to sit back and relax in self-satisfaction. Instead, we always will find more deficiencies and faults in ourselves to shoo away, more rough edges to smooth, more imperfections to refine toward greater perfection.

Why, then, should we choose to take up the twin burdens of fuller growth and total love? We can, as an alternative, simply sink into the society around us. We can go with the flow, accept modern life and love as they are, enjoy the highs and suffer the lows, accept and endure shattered romances, broken marriages, fragmented religion, and fractured lives like so many other people around us.

An Oriental sage once observed that evil—which is best defined as something that harms life—can be sweet at first but turns increasingly bitter. In this we see clearly the course of stunted love: often sweet at first but ending in problems massive, brutal, and totally unacceptable. The sage also said that good—which is best defined as what benefits life— might begin with hardship but becomes increasingly sweet. So goes the course of healthy growth and benevolent love: often difficult at first but easier and happier as they move along.

This clarifies the choice between low life and growing life, partial love and total love. It stresses that when we choose our path we also choose consequences.

DECIDING TO LOVE

Effective love is well worth our trouble for simple practicality. It is as vital as food and drink to sustain life in the overall plan of human existence. Love is not only a process but a dynamic power. It is curative and creative. We need to love and to be loved for emotional, mental, and physical health—for anything beyond a minimal degree of personal and social survival.

The French novelist Albert Camus wrote, "There is merely bad luck in not being loved; there is tragedy in not loving. All of us, today, are dying of this tragedy." He meant, of course, a metaphorical death, an atrophy of heart, a decay of soul. Yet human beings also literally can die from lack of love.

In the 1950s, the anthropologist M. F. Ashley Montagu wrote in *The Direction of Human Development*, "What the human organism requires most for its development is a nutriment of love; the source of virtually all health is in the experience of love, especially within the first six years of life. No matter how well the needs of the human organism are physically satisfied, unless the physical satisfying of those needs is accompanied by love, the human organism will not develop satisfactorily." He went on to cite numerous studies of infants languishing for lack of emotional nurture. Their debility, often fatal, is considered a disease and is known as infantile atrophy, or marasmus, from the Greek word meaning "wasting away."

In the 1990s I witness horrifying examples of this condition when I traveled on a journalistic assignment through Romania. A cold-hearted communist dictatorship had fallen, and the world learned of ghastly orphanages where nearly 100,000 children existed without sufficient food, clothing, heat, and most of all, human attention.

In dark and dank dormitory rooms staffed by only a few untrained workers, I saw row upon row of steel-barred cribs where children as old as four and five had spent their entire lives. Sheets and mattresses stank of foulness. Diapers were changed perfunctorily on fixed schedule, with no regard for need.

No one talked to these children or spent time with them. They were told no stories, sung no songs, not taught to play any games. Many could not talk or walk. Four-year-olds, failing to grow physically as well as emotionally, looked like infants. Other children stood, hands gripping cold bars, and rocked back and forth for hours at a time, the only stimulation they knew. If anybody tried to pick up these little ones, they would shrink from human touch and scream. Such a thing never had happened to them before. Death in these institutions was not unusual.

One of my colleagues and his wife adopted a five-year-old girl named Elena from one of these orphanages. Later she told her parents she had felt terribly cold in her crib with only one thin blanket. But she had experienced no emotions: she was never sad, never happy, never anything.

Just as infants need love to grow in every way, older children need it for a sense of their identity. A few years after Romania, I was traveling through the Central African country of Rwanda in the aftermath of a genocidal slaughter of an estimated 800,000 people. I saw many children orphaned or lost during the mass killings. Some were found amid piles of corpses and rescued. Many wore great scars from attempts to bludgeon them or hack them to death with machetes. One little boy whose parents were lost or killed, when asked his name, said only, "I am nobody's nothing."

Though we think of adults as largely independent, they also need the benefits of love if they are to thrive. Medical doctor Dean Ornish, in his book *Love & Survival*, revealed dozens of studies showing solitary people with a vastly greater rate of premature death than people with ties to family and community. He added: "Indeed, several books have been written summarizing the scientific and medical literature on the health-damaging consequences of loneliness and isolation and the life-enhancing power of love and intimacy."

Zoologist and author Desmond Morris writes about our own society: "In a social environment that is ever more crowded and impersonal, it is becoming increasingly important to reconsider the value of close personal relationships before we are driven to ask the forlorn question, 'Whatever happened to love?'" A large part of this value in personal relationships lies in successfully building and maintaining our own emotional well-being.

Love of one sort or another is necessary simply for mental-emotional health. Sanity depends on our contact with the world beyond the self, on establishing and maintaining a relationship between the self and what lies beyond. Any person who seriously fails in this task loses reality and dwells in one or another form of insanity, whether fantasies, hallucinations, delusions, or withdrawal.

Just as we may choose between three basic modes of love, so can we choose among three general ways to come out of the self and establish contact with the world beyond:

✦ The infant's way is to receive and take, which in terms of love translates as eros. Life gets along, even thrives temporarily, when it feeds off other life. Yet this method leaves a person dependent and weak—or strong only through consuming and destroying. People beyond infancy who follow this course wither and decay spiritually and emotionally. If somehow their external sources of life are withdrawn, they collapse.

✦ The child's way is to judiciously swap and conserve, in the manner of lower-level philia. A reasonably successful life—though still profoundly incomplete—can be built on formal and informal contractual relationships that resemble trade and commerce.

✦ The adult way is to reach beyond the self in giving, serving, agape-loving— to "put oneself out," as the phrase goes. People who work at this method develop spiritual soundness, emotional strength, and healthy personal independence.

The natural pattern of healthy human growth leads from mainly consuming as infants, to increasingly producing or creating as maturing people. As we progress in our lives from one level of maturity to the next, our focus of perception shifts ever more from self to the world outside the self. People who remain at the infantile level sink into a narcissistic tomb. Those who grow highest on the scale of maturity soar into sainthood.

Meanwhile, higher-level loving relationships are vital to our life's enrichment. Just as existence among hostile or disparaging people can suppress our personality and diminish our abilities, so can generous love nurture a flowering of personhood that nothing else can achieve. By giving of ourselves, we become more fulfilled. By receiving love, we are strengthened all the more. In mutual love we cease to be separate and become part of a larger, stronger human unit known as "we." At the same time, paradoxically, as we participate in effective love we develop far better individually as "I."

In loving and being loved at a higher level of love, we can function more effectively in all our relationships. We feel fortified and freer to reveal ourselves. We are more confident and outgoing, more trusting and secure, more aware of our human potential. Love fills us with new energy, boosts our interest in living, gives us fresh eagerness to strive toward higher goals and ideals. Meanwhile, we find great freedom in love—the only service that power cannot command. We also find in love one of life's few absolute securities: Our growing in love is the only continuity we can be sure of controlling and possessing eternally.

Should we bear old injuries of heart, as certainly the children I saw in Romania and Rwanda did, love will serve to make us whole. "Love cures people, both the ones who give it and the ones who receive it," assured Dr. Karl Menninger of the psychiatric clinic that bears his family name.

The fifth-century BC Chinese sage Confucius pointed out how love ripples through all society. "When there is love in the home," he observed, "there is peace in the kingdom." Love is the origin and preserver of goodness and life. Love is the bond of generations, the bridge between life and death, the cement of society, the security of civilization, the only foundation of the human future.

The great religions of humankind speak of the enormous importance and significance of love. Buddhism tells of the Bodhisattvas who deny themselves the bliss of Nirvana in order to help others find fulfillment. Many Hindus worship a savior god Ganesha who represents the soul of compassion. Followers of Islam speak of Allah as the all-merciful and compassionate God, while the faith's Sufi saints refer to a mysticism of love. In Confucianism and Taoism, compassion and caring are part of pursuing the Way of Tao. The I Ching speaks of the creative life as characterized by quiet, humble, unobtrusive concern for others. Hasidic Judaism offers profound wisdom on the value and importance of love. In Christianity, love is the central point and purpose of divine and human existence.

Jesus explained that we should love one another not only for the joy it brings and the good it creates. We should love, too, because in doing so we share in the very nature of God, who at once loves and is love. By loving we can come to know God and to dwell in his kingdom, not only in an afterlife but now, immediately, increasingly. "All the way to heaven is heaven," observed St. Catherine of Siena.

The German theologian Paul Tillich wrote that love "is life itself in its actual unity." The forms and structures in which love embodies itself are the same forms and structures in which life overcomes its self-destructive forces. The simple commandment of Jesus to "love one another," if it were practiced by many people, would change the world everywhere in everything, diminishing misery, removing poverty, closing prisons.

Though we cannot depend upon other people to work out this magnificent goal, your love and mine can change our part of this world. When we accept the considerable tasks of growing and rising to effective love, we personally find that embracing good might begin with hardship but unfailingly turns ever-sweeter.

Rising to Love   16

IN LOVE EVERY MAN STARTS FROM THE BEGINNING.
—SØREN KIERKEGAARD (1813–1855)

W E HAVE THE UNIQUE OPPORTUNITY to reinvent the ways of
love. Instead of only falling in love, we also can rise to love.
   The society at large will not tell us much about how to ascend above
eros. Rather it tends to influence us to cling to baby-love. The mass
media especially promotes and induces a low, ineffective, often sickly
level of eros. Genuine philia-love is little known and less compre-
hended, so no one can help us much with that. Agape is positively alien,
seen at once as laudable, unusual, perilous, and practiced mainly by
spiritual geniuses or fools. In such a social atmosphere, when we set
out to build total love in our own lives, each of us must start from the
beginning.

WHO CAN LOVE?

Anyone can do it. Every person alive has a capacity for total love. The
aptitude for all three levels of love is born into us, though it must be
developed just as any other human ability.
   The inborn nature of eros, with its quest for self-fulfillment, is obvious. Every baby wants and needs, then coos sweetly when satisfied.
Some theories of child development claim that infants stop there, incapable of acting as anything more than bundles of desire. Hinging on
Freud's idea of the superego—that morality is wholly nurtured rather
than naturally seeded—and studies done by the Swiss child psychologist Jean Piaget, these theories claim that young children until the age

of five or six are completely self-centered and have no capacity for altruistic feeling.

Other psychologists say otherwise, as do many perceptive parents. They observe infants displaying shoots of higher love from their earliest months. Who has not seen small children offering grateful smiles, joyful hugs, flowers pulled from the grass, drawings of stick figures?

Wrote physician and psychologist Franz E. Winkler: ". . . when the child senses that the care given to him is unselfish, his innate tendency to reciprocate begins to unfold at a very early age. So early indeed that an experienced psychologist can get a pretty good idea of the parental attitude from the facial expression and emotional response of a six-month old. Owing to his physical limitations, the child cannot offer material compensation for the care he receives; but seeking recourse in the world of qualitative values, he can reward his parents with gratitude and love."

Psychologists at the Laboratory of Developmental Psychology, part of the United States National Institute of Mental Health, determined in a detailed study that babies and small children often behave with surprising altruism:

+ An eighteen-month-old girl sees her grandmother lie down and toddles to her crib, gets her own blanket, and covers the woman.
+ The family dog sneezes and an eighteen-month-old boy runs for a tissue to wipe the animal's nose.
+ A fifteen-month-old boy, seeing his mother tired, pats her tenderly and offers her his bottle.
+ A two-year-old boy accidentally hits a little girl on the head. "I hurt your hair," he tells her in dismay. "Please don't cry."

The study's data showed clearly that children are capable of positive social behavior and compassion from at least the age of one.

A summary of childhood development studies revealed that children one to two years old frequently respond to the distress of others with agitation. By twenty-four months they often will try to comfort an apparently suffering person with verbal sympathy and objects they believe might help. While small children are not capable of deep and sustained altruistic love, its elements are present and waiting to be developed.

Once we accept that higher love is built into our nature, we have nothing left to do but begin to develop it. What do we do first? The seventeenth-century French churchman St. Francis de Sales advised, "You learn to speak by speaking, to study by studying, to run by running, to work by working; and just so you learn to love God and man by loving. Begin as a mere apprentice, and the very power of love will lead you on to become a master of the art."

Confucius taught that each of us can develop benevolence by practicing empathy—putting ourselves in the position of others then dealing with them as we would like to be treated. "Do not do to others what you would not like yourself," he advised. He added to this version of the Golden Rule: "Do unto others what you wish to do unto yourself."

And what is the best course of action for people who are looking for love? The formula is the same: to have it, do it. Or in the words of the sixteenth-century Spanish mystic and poet St. John of the Cross, "Where there is no love, put love, and there you will find love." Anyone who would complicate the matter further is evading love.

Not that we should expect to soar instantly to lofty heights of altruism. If we leap too hard we will only end up straining ourselves or mimicking love's outward appearances. We must mature into love, growing from the inside out. This takes time, much attention, effort, wisdom, even planning, as with any other kind of human growth. We will not arrive at love's higher levels right away, but gradually, by practice, with day-by-day and year-by-year progress in emotional and spiritual maturity.

Growth is the key to success here. We climb the steps of love and grow emotionally—just as we grow physically and intellectually—one intentional effort at a time.

Imagine the rising scale of love, with eros rooted on earth and the highest agape-love infinitely above our reach in the realm of the divine. Since we, too, are on earth with eros we never leave it altogether behind, nor should we because eros at its best is our impetus for growth. Yet in every effort to grow we reach higher toward agape-love, and this very stretching makes us bigger and stronger so we can reach higher still.

As we grow, our personal understanding of love shifts from focus on self to focus on others, from egocentricity to generosity, from passive to active, from a tickle in the tummy or an amiable feeling to actions of service for the welfare of whomever we love.

What level am I living and loving on now? That is the question to begin with. If it is less than agape, which is almost certain in our emotionally retarded society, then I must live carefully and constructively at my level of love so I can grow to higher levels.

Consider low-level, baby-love eros, for example, since that causes the most trouble in our society. Many people presently suffer terrible consequences from being stuck at this deficient level of love. So how can eros be turned into a positive experience?

We all see that eros, if not growing and surpassing itself, flames out in self-destruction. So how can we assure love after romance? To keep love alive after eros has finished swirling us up in its vortex, we must help it grow up. Rather than squandering its thrilling motivation solely on our pleasure, we can use its impetus, as it undoubtedly was meant by nature to be used, as an investment in higher love.

Eros at its best can inspire a magnificent overleaping of base selfishness. Suddenly we are able to cast aside even personal happiness and make appetite itself altruistic in spontaneous and effortless loving of another as oneself. When we use the fuel of eros to empower kindness, generosity, consideration, and care, then our delirious happiness in beginner's love becomes a foretaste of the splendors and joys of higher love even before they are earned.

How can we guarantee our growing? In two words: Reach high. In more words: Be as generous as possible as often as possible. Promise the moon if you like, but shoot for the moon as well. Make serving the greatest good of another the major goal of love. Work toward the highest love, and the other levels of love will take care of themselves as we rise on the sheer momentum of earnest benevolence.

The various levels of love are in no way restricted to people presently living mainly at those levels. Eros is not only for beginners, nor philia only for people of mid-development, nor agape only for great humanitarians and saints. Anyone might love at any level at any moment.

Nor does one level of love predominating in us ever exclude another completely. All three levels stir within us simultaneously all our lives. They change only in proportion. One slips into the background as another moves into the foreground. In a life of healthy spiritual-emotional growth, gradually the copper of eros is overlaid with the silver of philia and, when we grow beyond that, the two are dazzlingly plated with agape's gold.

LOVE AS EFFORT

Rising in love is work, of course. It is cleansing, wonderfully satisfying, often pleasant, but work all the same. It demands that we develop inner disciplines. It requires that we strive for self-control in mastering desires, passions, and instincts. We must train ourselves to honesty in word and implication. We must be faithful in keeping promises and fulfilling responsibilities. We must tame both weaknesses and strengths so we actually can do what we intend to accomplish. Only as we gain reasonable governance over self can we give ourselves effectively in service to others.

Restoring an ethical basis for love allows its most important element—care—to move into action. "So you are in love . . ." old books on love began. Yet they neglected to ask: "Is love in you?"

The care that love needs for its development reaches far beyond passive sentiment. The Russian novelist Leo Tolstoy wrote of wealthy women in a theater weeping maudlin tears for the plight of characters on stage while feeling nothing but indifference for their coachmen shivering in bitter cold outside the theater. Their tender feelings were wholly self-centered, affecting other people no more than did the state of their digestion.

The care of higher love might be an internal feeling but it also must express itself with external action. This care flows outside the self to wish someone well and then is willing to do something about it. Is there a person in our lives whose growth and well-being is as important to us as our own satisfactions? Do we sense this person as a distinct human being with value of her or his own, as opposed to the person's instrumental value for our use or pleasure? If so, we have found higher love—not *out there*, but in ourselves.

Nothing less than the warmth of active care can bring renewed human meaning to the vast impersonal emptiness of modern existence. One of the great tragedies of the present is a common feeling of apathy. This life-denying emotional affliction is expressed in a creeping suspicion that nothing really matters because in the end everything is meaningless. The caring of higher love is its cure. The German philosopher Martin Heidegger writes of care as "the basic constitutive phenomenon of human existence."

At first thought, in an age when lower love predominates, virtuous and controlled love might seem hard to assent to and even harder to accomplish. And so it is! But, again, what kind of growth is not difficult? Emotional progress is no less demanding than muscle-building or studying for a degree. Yet, in the final analysis, it is infinitely more rewarding than either.

And how does this kind of disciplined love work in romance? It works very well indeed! In due and pleasant time, a kind, considerate romance—as in days when romance was still sweet—lifts romancers upward to true happy friendship. I do not mean the pallid, on-and-off acquaintance or mutual using that passes for friendship in our cool-hearted age, but the deep, warm, enduring devotion of people who cherish one another and eagerly help each other live well.

Then, when exercise in philia's generosities, consideration, and kindness brings still more emotional growth, the fuller giving of agape begins to flow like grace, with its tender selflessness, noble sacrifices, and joy in promoting the highest welfare of others.

So, whether in romance or in other relationships, the three levels of love—at its opposite ends, self-serving and self-giving—lead us upward as stepping stones. Anyone who follows them grows from emotional infantilism to maturity, from self-absorption to liberation from the self's demands, from spiritual poverty to gracious inner wealth.

As we love in this conscious and maturing way, we see love less as a matter of attraction and more as a decision. We come to understand it as no mere pleasurable feeling or passive emotion, but as a dynamic act of will, a deliberate choice of generosity, self-control, and, in our society, considerable courage. We realize, then, that falling in love is nothing, and rising to love is everything.

Since we never grow entirely beyond the lesser loves, we shall go on wanting and needing and seeking self-fulfillment in some way as long as we live. Nor can or should we ever leave behind philia. The first two levels of love, remaining within us always, are not merely residues of our past but worthy and valuable parts of our emotional being. Then, when these lesser loves are guided by the highest love of agape, we continue to grow and thrive by way of healthy exercise. In time we rise to levels of emotional maturity where agape-love becomes no longer a task but an easy and joyous way of living.

LOVE'S ECONOMY

At first, total love seems impossibly costly, but its economy turns out to be totally miraculous. Love does not exist until you give it away. It spends its all and still has more in store. The more we produce, the more we are capable of producing. The more we give, the more we have, and the more comes back to us. Love is the only treasure that multiplies by division, the only business where it pays to be a spendthrift. We can give it away, empty our pockets, tip our cup upside down, and we find that we have more than we ever had before.

Once we practice total love, we find people around us seeking it, too. Just as spiritual sickness is contagious, spiritual health energizes and inspires. Anyone can understand love, which is not taught by words so much as caught by example. Love communicates to everyone everywhere without the need for language, belief in a creed, or even faith.

Nor does the value of love ever change, regardless of place or time. Listen to its witnesses across the ages. They speak to us today:

> "Love slays what we have been that we may be what we were not." —theologian St. Augustine of Hippo (354–430)

> "Love makes a subtle man out of a crude one, it gives eloquence to the mute; it gives courage to the cowardly; and

makes the idle quick and sharp." —Spanish poet Juan Ruiz (1283–1350)

"Love makes all hard hearts gentle." —English metaphysical poet George Herbert (1593–1633)

"Love is a symbol of eternity. It wipes out all sense of time, destroying all memory of a beginning and all fear of an end." —French-Swiss writer Germaine de Staël (1766–1817)

"Love makes the whole difference between an execution and a martyrdom." —English writer and mystic Evelyn Underhill (1875–1941)

"We have all been created for the same purpose . . . to love and be loved." —Albanian-born Roman Catholic missionary and Nobel laureate Mother Teresa of Calcutta (1910–1997)

"In the evening of life, we will be judged on love alone." —Spanish mystic St. John of the Cross (1542–1591)

Bibliography and Further Reading

Ackerman, Diane. *A Natural History of Love.* New York: Random House, 1994.

Arieti, Silvano, and James A. Arieti. *Love Can Be Found.* New York: Harcourt Brace Jovanovich, 1977.

Bailey, Beth L. *From Front Porch to Back Seat.* Baltimore: Johns Hopkins University, 1988.

Beauvoir, Simone de. *The Second Sex.* Trans. and ed. by H. M. Parshley. New York: Vintage Books, 1989.

Berscheid, Ellen, and Elaine Hatfield Walster. *Interpersonal Attraction.* Reading, Mass.: Addison-Wesley, 1969.

Blankenhorn, David. *Fatherless America: Confronting Our Most Urgent Social Problem.* New York: Basic Books, 1995.

Bloom, Allan. *Love and Friendship.* New York: Simon & Schuster, 1993.

Bowlby, John. *Attachment and Loss.* Vol. 1, *Attachment.* New York: Basic Books, 1969.

Bradshaw, John. *Creating Love.* New York: Bantam, 1992.

Branden, Nathaniel. *The Psychology of Romantic Love.* Los Angeles: J. P. Tarcher, 1980.

Brothers, Joyce. *What Every Woman Should Know About Men.* New York: Simon and Schuster, 1981.

Burgess, Ernest W., and Leonard S. Cottrell. *Predicting Success or Failure in Marriage.* New York: Prentice-Hall, 1939.

Buscaglia, Leo. *Loving Each Other.* Thorofare, N.J.: Slack, 1984.

Callahan, Roger, with Karen Levine. *It Can Happen to You: The Practical Guide to Romantic Love.* New York: A & W Publishers, 1982.

Council on Families in America, "Marriage in America, A Report to the Nation." New York: Institute for American Values, 1995.

Cowell, F. R. *History, Civilization and Culture.* London: Thames and Hudson, 1952.

———. *Values in Human Society.* Boston: Porter Sargent, 1970.

Deyo, Yaacov, and Sue Deyo, *Speed Dating: The Smarter, Faster Way to Lasting Love.* New York: HarperResource, 2002.

Fisher, Helen E. *The Anatomy of Love.* New York: W. W. Norton, 1992.

Freud, Sigmund. "The Taboo of Virginity" (1918). In *Collected Papers*. Vol. 4. Trans. by Joan Riviere. New York: Basic Books, 1959.

———. "On the Universal Tendency to Debasement in the Sphere of Love" (1912), in *Standard Edition* of *The Complete Psychological Works of Sigmund Freud*. Trans. and ed. James Strachey. London: Hogarth Press, 1961.

Fromm, Eric. *The Art of Loving*. New York: Harper and Row, 1956.

———. *Escape from Freedom*. New York: Avon, 1965.

———. *Man for Himself*. New York: Fawcett, 1967.

———. *The Sane Society*. New York: Fawcett, 1955.

Gaylin, Willard. *Rediscovering Love*. New York: Viking, 1986.

Gelb, Norman. *The Irresistible Impulse*. New York: Paddington, 1979.

Glenn, Norval, and Elizabeth Marquardt (principal investigators). "Hooking Up, Hanging Out, and Hoping for Mr. Right: College Women on Dating and Mating Today." New York: Institute for American Values Report to the Independent Women's Forum, 2002.

Gottman, John. *Why Marriages Succeed or Fail*. New York: Simon and Schuster, 1994.

Halpern, Howard M. *How to Break Your Addiction to a Person*. New York: McGraw-Hill, 1982.

Harris, Joshua. *I Kissed Dating Goodbye*. Sisters, Ore.: Multnomah Publishers, 1997.

Hazo, Robert G. *The Idea of Love*. New York: Frederick A. Praeger, 1967.

Hendrick, Susan S., and Clyde Hendrick. *Romantic Love*. Newbury Park, Calif.: Sage Publications, 1992.

Hunt, Morton M. *The Natural History of Love*. New York: Alfred A. Knopf, 1959.

Jourard, Sidney M. *The Transparent Self*. Princeton, N.J.: D. Van Nostrand, 1964.

Keen, Sam. *To Love and Be Loved*. New York: Bantam Books, 1997.

———. *The Passionate Life*. New York: Harper and Row, 1983.

Kelsey, Morton T. *Caring: How Can We Love One Another?* New York: Paulist Press, 1981.

Kiefer, Otto. *Sexual Life in Ancient Rome*. London: Abbey Library, 1976.

Lasch, Christopher. *Women and the Common Life: Love, Marriage, and Feminism*. New York: W. W. Norton, 1997.

Lewis, C. S. *The Four Loves*. New York: Harcourt, Brace & World, 1960.

Lewis, Thomas, Fari Amini, and Richard Lannon. *A General Theory of Love*. New York: Random House, 2000.

Liebowitz, Michael R. *The Chemistry of Love*. Boston: Little, Brown, 1983.

Lyman, Stanford M. *The Seven Deadly Sins*. New York: St. Martin's Press, 1978.

Mace, David, and Vera Mace. *Marriage: East and West*. Garden City, N.Y.: Doubleday, 1960.

Mack, Dana, and David Blankenhorn, eds. *The Book of Marriage*. Grand Rapids, Mich.: William B. Eerdmans, 2001.

Martin, Mike W. *Love's Virtues*. Lawrence, Kans.: University Press of Kansas, 1996.

Matter, Joseph Allen. *Love, Altruism, and World Crisis: The Challenge of Pitirim Sorokin*. Chicago: Nelson-Hall, 1974.

May, Rollo. *Love and Will.* New York: W. W. Norton, 1969.

Merton, Thomas. *Love and Living.* New York: Bantam, 1980.

Mohler, James A., S.J. *Dimensions of Love East and West.* Garden City, N.Y.: Doubleday, 1975.

Monroe, Kristen Renwick. *The Heart of Altruism: Perceptions of a Common Humanity.* Princeton, N.J.: Princeton University Press, 1996.

Montagu, M. F. Ashley, ed. *The Meaning of Love.* New York: Julian Press, 1953.

————. *The Direction of Human Development.* New York: Harper, 1955.

Mumford, Lewis. *The Conduct of Life.* New York: Harcourt Brace Jovanovich, 1970.

Murstein, Bernard L. *Love, Sex and Marriage Through the Ages.* New York: Springer, 1974.

Myers, David G. *The American Paradox: Spiritual Hunger in An Age of Plenty.* New Haven, Conn.: Yale University Press, 2000.

Nordau, Max. *Degeneration.* New York: Appleton, 1895.

Nouwen, Henri J. M. *The Life of the Beloved.* New York: Crossroad, 1992.

Nygren, Anders. *Agape and Eros.* Trans. by Philip S. Watson. Philadelphia: Westminster Press, 1953.

Ornish, Dean. *Love and Survival.* New York: HarperCollins, 1998.

Overstreet, Harry. *The Mature Mind.* New York: W. W. Norton, 1949.

Parrott, Les, and Leslie Parrott. *Saving Your Marriage before It Starts: Seven Questions to Ask Before (and After) You Marry.* Grand Rapids, Mich.: Zondervan, 1995.

Peele, Stanton, with Archie Brodsky. *Love and Addiction.* New York: Signet, New American Library Penguin, 1975.

Plato. *The Symposium.* In *Great Books of the Western World.* Chicago: Encyclopedia Britannica, 1971.

Post, Stephen G. *Unlimited Love: Altruism, Compassion, and Service.* Philadelphia: Templeton Foundation Press, 2003.

Post, Stephen G., Lynn G. Underwood, Jeffrey P. Schloss, and William B. Hurlburt, eds. *Altruism and Altruistic Love: Science, Philosophy, and Religion in Dialogue.* New York and Oxford: Oxford University Press, 2002.

Reik, Theodore. *Of Love and Lust.* New York: Farrar, Straus and Cudahy, 1957.

Rossi, Alice S. *Caring and Doing for Others: Social Responsibility in the Domains of Family, Work, and Community.* Chicago: University of Chicago Press, 2001.

Rougemont, Denis de. *Love in the Western World.* New York: Pantheon, 1956.

Rubin, Theodore. *Real Love.* New York: Continuum, 1990.

Scanzoni, Letha, and John Scanzoni. *Men, Women and Change: A Sociology of Marriage and Family.* New York: McGraw-Hill, 1976.

Shalit, Wendy. *A Return to Modesty: Discovering the Lost Virtue.* New York: Free Press, 1999.

Short, Ray E. *Sex, Love or Infatuation: How Can I Really Know?* Minneapolis: Augsburg, 1978.

Singer, Irving. *The Nature of Love*. 3 vols. Chicago: University of Chicago Press, 1984–1987.

Smith, Tom W. "American Sexual Behavior: Trends, Socio-Demographic Differences, and Risk Behavior." National Opinion Research Center, University of Chicago, 2003.

Solomon, Robert C. *About Love*. Lanham, Md.: Rowman and Littelefield, 1994.

———. *Love: Emotion, Myth and Metaphor*. New York: Anchor Press/Doubleday, 1981.

Sorokin, Pitirim A., ed. *Explorations in Altruistic Love and Behavior*. Boston: Beacon, 1950.

———. *Social and Cultural Dynamics*, ab. Boston: Porter Sargent, 1957.

———. *The Ways and Power of Love*. Philadelphia: Templeton Foundation Press, 2002 [1954].

Stendhal, Marie-Henri Beyle de. *On Love*. New York: Da Capo, 1983.

Swidler, Ann. *Talk of Love: How Culture Matters*. Chicago: University of Chicago Press, 2001.

Tannahill, Reay. *Sex in History*. New York: Stein and Day, 1980.

Templeton, Sir John. *Agape Love: A Tradition Found in Eight World Religions*. Philadelphia: Templeton Foundation Press, 1999.

———. *Pure Unlimited Love*. Philadelphia: Templeton Foundation Press, 2000.

Tennov, Dorothy. *Love and Limerence: The Experience of Being in Love*. New York: Stein and Day, 1979.

Tweedie, Jill. *In the Name of Love*. New York: Pantheon, 1979.

Unwin, J. D. *Sex and Culture*. London: Oxford University Press, 1934.

Waite, Linda J. *The Ties That Bind: Perspectives on Marriage and Cohabitation*. New York: Aldine de Gruyter, 2000.

Waite, Linda J., and Maggie Gallagher. *The Case for Marriage: Why Married People are Happier, Healthier, and Better Off Financially*. New York: Doubleday, 2000.

Walsh, Anthony. *The Science of Love*. Buffalo: Prometheus, 1991.

Walster, Elaine, and G. William Walster. *A New Look at Love*. Reading, Mass.: Addison-Wesley, 1978.

Whitehead, Barbara Dafoe. *The Divorce Culture*. New York: Alfred A. Knopf, 1997.

———. *Why There Are No Good Men Left: The Romantic Plight of the New Single Woman*. New York: Broadway Books, 2003.

Why Marriage Matters: 21 Conclusions from the Social Sciences. New York: Center of the American Experiment, Coalition of Marriage, Family and Couples Education, 2002.

Williamson, Marianne. *A Return to Love*. New York: HarperCollins, 1992.

Winkler, Franz E. *Man: The Bridge Between Two Worlds*. Garden City, N.Y.: Waldorf Press, 1960.

Index

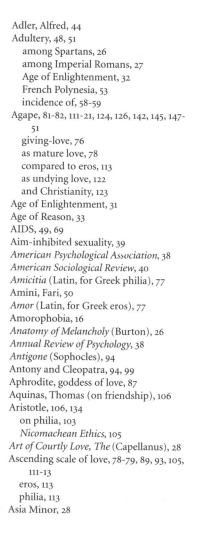

About the Author

Bruce Brander is an international journalist, independent scholar, award-winning photographer, teacher, and author of six books on travel and social philosophy. He has worked on the staffs of newspapers in New Zealand and the United States and was a writer and editor for National Geographic. Brander has taught in the field of communications in the United States and abroad, and for twelve years served as traveling journalist and editor for World Vision, a global relief and development agency.

His continuing studies of social and cultural trends in the modern Western world involve sociology, psychology, history, anthropology, and current events. His last book, *Staring into Chaos*, involves world history and grand theory sociology regarding the formation, life-course, and decline of more than twenty-four civilizations.

Brander became interested in the subject of love at the age of twenty-two, when he entered university after four years of travel as a merchant seaman and soldier. Ready to marry and settle down, he wisely doubted the validity of our society's ideas about love, but unwisely followed them anyway. After a few distressing romances, he set out to learn all he could about what love is and how to make it work in the hope of helping other people as well as himself. His studies on the subject began more than thirty years ago and became the subject of this book.

As a testimony to what he learned, he has been married to his wife, Mary, for more than nineteen years, and they have a happy and congenial family with four children, ages twelve to seventeen. They reside in Colorado.